Fifine At the Fair by Robert Browning

Robert Browning is one of the most significant Victorian Poets and, of course, English Poetry.

Much of his reputation is based upon his mastery of the dramatic monologue although his talents encompassed verse plays and even a well-regarded essay on Shelley during a long and prolific career.

He was born on May 7th, 1812 in Walmouth, London. Much of his education was home based and Browning was an eclectic and studious student, learning several languages and much else across a myriad of subjects, interests and passions.

Browning's early career began promisingly. The fragment from his intended long poem Pauline brought him to the attention of Dante Gabriel Rossetti, and was followed by Paracelsus, which was praised by both William Wordsworth and Charles Dickens. In 1840 the difficult Sordello, which was seen as willfully obscure, brought his career almost to a standstill.

Despite these artistic and professional difficulties his personal life was about to become immensely fulfilling. He began a relationship with, and then married, the older and better known Elizabeth Barrett. This new foundation served to energise his writings, his life and his career.

During their time in Italy they both wrote much of their best work. With her untimely death in 1861 he returned to London and thereafter began several further major projects.

The collection Dramatis Personae (1864) and the book-length epic poem The Ring and the Book (1868-69) were published and well received; his reputation as a venerated English poet now assured.

Robert Browning died in Venice on December 12th, 1889.

Index of Contents

FIFINE AT THE FAIR

DONE ELVIRE
Vous plaît-il, don Juan, nous éclaircir ces beaux mystères?

DON JUAN

Madame, à vous dire la vérité...

DONE ELVIRE

Ah! que vous savez mal vous défendre pour un homme de cour, et qui doit être accoutumé à ces sortes de choses! J'ai pitié de vous voir la confusion que vous avez. Que ne vous armez-vous le front d'une noble effronterie? Que ne me jurez-vous que vous êtes toujours dans les mêmes sentimens pour moi, que vous m'aimez toujours avec une ardeur sans égale, et que rien n'est capable de vous detacher de moi que la mort?—(MOLIERE, Don Juan, Acte i, Sc 3.)

DONNA ELVIRA

Don Juan, might you please to help one give a guess,
Hold up a candle, clear this fine mysteriousness?

DON JUAN

Madam, if needs I must declare the truth,—in short ...

DONNA ELVIRA

Fie, for a man of mode, accustomed at the court
To such a style of thing, how awkwardly my lord
Attempts defence! You move compassion, that's the word—
Dumb-foundered and chapfallen! Why don't you arm your brow
With noble impudence? Why don't you swear and vow
No sort of change is come to any sentiment
You ever had for me? Affection holds the bent,
You love me now as erst, with passion that makes pale
All ardor else: nor aught in nature can avail
To separate us two, save what, in stopping breath,
May peradventure stop devotion likewise—death!

PROLOGUE

AMPHIBIAN

The fancy I had to-day,
Fancy which turned a fear!
I swam far out in the bay,
Since waves laughed warm and clear.

I lay and looked at the sun,
The noon-sun looked at me:
Between us two, no one
Live creature, that I could see.

Yes! There came floating by
Me, who lay floating too,
Such a strange butterfly!

Creature as dear as new:

Because the membraned wings
So wonderful, so wide,
So sun-suffused, were things
Like soul and naught beside.

A handbreadth overhead!
All of the sea my own,
It owned the sky instead;
Both of us were alone.

I never shall join its flight,
For, naught buoys flesh in air.
If it touch the sea—good night!
Death sure and swift waits there.

Can the insect feel the better
For watching the uncouth play
Of limbs that slip the fetter,
Pretend as they were not clay?

Undoubtedly I rejoice
That the air comports so well
With a creature which had the choice
Of the land once. Who can tell?

What if a certain soul
Which early slipped its sheath,
And has for its home the whole
Of heaven, thus look beneath,

Thus watch one who, in the world,
Both lives and likes life's way,
Nor wishes the wings unfurled
That sleep in the worm, they say?

But sometimes when the weather
Is blue, and warm waves tempt
To free one's self of tether,
And try a life exempt

From worldly noise and dust,
In the sphere which overbrims
With passion and thought,—why, just
Unable to fly, one swims!

By passion and thought upborne,

One smiles to one's self—"They fare
Scarce better, they need not scorn
Our sea, who live in the air!"

Emancipate through passion
And thought, with sea for sky,
We substitute, in a fashion,
For heaven—poetry:

Which sea, to all intent,
Gives flesh such noon-disport
As a finer element
Affords the spirit-sort.

Whatever they are, we seem:
Imagine the thing they know;
All deeds they do, we dream;
Can heaven be else but so?

And meantime, yonder streak
Meets the horizon's verge;
That is the land, to seek
If we tire or dread the surge:

Land the solid and safe—
To welcome again (confess!)
When, high and dry, we chafe
The body, and don the dress.

Does she look, pity, wonder
At one who mimics flight,
Swims—heaven above, sea under,
Yet always earth in sight?

FIFINE AT THE FAIR

I

O trip and skip, Elvire! Link arm in arm with me!
Like husband and like wife, together let us see
The tumbling-troop arrayed, the strollers on their stage,
Drawn up and under arms, and ready to engage.

II

Now, who supposed the night would play us such a prank?
—That what was raw and brown, rough pole and shaven plank,
Mere bit of hoarding, half by trestle propped, half tub,
Would flaunt it forth as brisk as butterfly from grub?
This comes of sun and air, of Autumn afternoon,
And Pornic and Saint Gille, whose feast affords the boon—
This scaffold turned parterre, this flower-bed in full blow,
Bateleurs, baladines! We shall not miss the show!
They pace and promenade; they presently will dance:
What good were else i' the drum and fife? O pleasant land of France!

III

Who saw them make their entry? At wink of eve, be sure!
They love to steal a march, nor lightly risk the lure.
They keep their treasure hid, nor stale (improvident)
Before the time is ripe, each wonder of their tent—
Yon six-legged sheep, to wit, and he who beats a gong,
Lifts cap and waves salute, exhilarates the throng—
Their ape of many years and much adventure, grim
And gray with pitying fools who find a joke in him.
Or, best, the human beauty, Mimi, Toinette, Fifine,
Tricot fines down if fat, padding plumps up if lean,
Ere, shedding petticoat, modesty, and such toys,
They bounce forth, squalid girls transformed to gamesome boys.

IV

No, no, thrice, Pornic, no! Perpend the authentic tale!
'T was not for every Gawain to gaze upon the Grail!
But whoso went his rounds, when flew bat, flitted midge,
Might hear across the dusk,—where both roads join the bridge,
Hard by the little port,—creak a slow caravan,
A chimneyed house on wheels; so shyly-sheathed, began
To broaden out the bud which, bursting unaware,
Now takes away our breath, queen-tulip of the Fair!

V

Yet morning promised much: for, pitched and slung and reared
On terrace 'neath the tower, 'twixt tree and tree appeared
An airy structure; how the pennon from its dome,
Frenetic to be free, makes one red stretch for home!
The home far and away, the distance where lives joy,
The cure, at once and ever, of world and world's annoy;

Since, what lolls full in front, a furlong from the booth,
But ocean-idleness, sky-blue and millpond-smooth?

Frenetic to be free! And, do you know, there beats
Something within my breast, as sensitive?—repeats
The fever of the flag? My heart makes just the same
Passionate stretch, fires up for lawlessness, lays claim
To share the life they lead: losels, who have and use
The hour what way they will,—applaud them or abuse
Society, whereof myself am at the beck,
Whose call obey, and stoop to burden stiffest neck!

Why is it that whene'er a faithful few combine
To cast allegiance off, play truant, nor repine,
Agree to bear the worst, forego the best in store
For us who, left behind, do duty as of yore,—
Why is it that, disgraced, they seem to relish life the more?
—Seem as they said, "We know a secret passing praise
Or blame of such as you! Remain! we go our ways
With something you o'erlooked, forgot or chose to sweep
Clean out of door: our pearl picked from your rubbish-heap.
You care not for your loss, we calculate our gain.
All 's right. Are you content? Why, so let things remain!
To the wood then, to the wild: free life, full liberty!"
And when they rendezvous beneath the inclement sky,
House by the hedge, reduced to brute-companionship,
—Misguided ones who gave society the slip,
And find too late how boon a parent they despised,
What ministration spurned, how sweet and civilized—
Then, left alone at last with self-sought wretchedness,
No interloper else!—why is it, can we guess?—
At somebody's expense, goes up so frank a laugh?
As though they held the corn, and left us only chaff
From garners crammed and closed. And we indeed are clever
If we get grain as good, by threshing straw forever!

Still, truants as they are and purpose yet to be,
That nowise needs forbid they venture—as you see—
To cross confine, approach the once familiar roof

O' the kindly race their flight estranged: stand half aloof,
Sidle half up, press near, and proffer wares for sale
—In their phrase,—make in ours, white levy of black mail.
They, of the wild, require some touch of us the tame,
Since clothing, meat and drink, mean money all the same.

IX

If hunger, proverbs say, allures the wolf from wood,
Much more the bird must dare a dash at something good:
Must snatch up, bear away in beak, the trifle-treasure
To wood and wild, and then—oh, how enjoy at leisure!
Was never tree-built nest, you climbed and took, of bird,
(Rare city-visitant, talked of, scarce seen or heard,)
But, when you would dissect the structure, piece by piece,
You found, enwreathed amid the country-product —fleece
And feather, thistle-fluffs and bearded windle-straws
Some shred of foreign silk, unravelling of gauze,
Bit, maybe, of brocade, mid fur and blow-bell-down:
Filched plainly from mankind, dear tribute paid by town,
Which proved how oft the bird had plucked up heart of grace,
Swooped down at waif and stray, made furtively our place
Pay tax and toll, then borne the booty to enrich
Her paradise i' the waste; the how and why of which,
That is the secret, there the mystery that stings!

X

For, what they traffic in, consists of just the things
We,—proud ones who so scorn dwellers without the pale,
Bateleurs, baladines, white leviers of black mail,
I say, they sell what we most pique us that we keep!
How comes it, all we hold so dear they count so cheap?

XI

What price should you impose, for instance, on repute,
Good fame, your own good fame and family's to boot?
Stay start of quick moustache, arrest the angry rise
Of eyebrow! All I asked is answered by surprise.
Now tell me: are you worth the cost of a cigar?
Go boldly, enter booth, disburse the coin at bar
Of doorway where presides the master of the troop,
And forthwith you survey his Graces in a group,
Live Picture, picturesque no doubt and close to life:

His sisters, right and left; the Grace in front, his wife.
Next, who is this performs the feat of the Trapeze?
Lo, she is launched, look—fie, the fairy!—how she flees
O'er all those heads thrust back,—mouths, eyes, one gape and stare,—
No scrap of skirt impedes free passage through the air,
Till, plumb on the other side, she lights and laughs again,
That fairy-form, whereof each muscle, nay, each vein
The curious may inspect,—his daughter that he sells
Each rustic for five sous. Desiderate aught else
O' the vendor? As you leave his show, why, joke the man!
"You cheat: your six-legged sheep, I recollect, began
Both life and trade, last year, trimmed properly and clipt,
As the Twin-headed Babe, and Human Nondescript!"
What does he care? You paid his price, may pass your jest.
So values he repute, good fame, and all the rest!

XII

But try another tack; say: "I indulge caprice,
Who am Don and Duke, and Knight, beside, o' the Golden Fleece,
And, never mind how rich. Abandon this career!
Have hearth and home, nor let your womankind appear
Without as multiplied a coating as protects
An onion from the eye! Become, in all respects,
God-fearing householder, subsistent by brain-skill,
Hand-labor; win your bread whatever way you will,
So it be honestly,—and, while I have a purse,
Means shall not lack!"—his thanks will be the roundest curse
That ever rolled from lip.

XIII

Now, what is it?—returns
The question—heartens so this losel that he spurns
All we so prize? I want, put down in black and white,
What compensating joy, unknown and infinite,
Turns lawlessness to law, makes destitution—wealth,
Vice—virtue, and disease of soul and body—health?

XIV

Ah, the slow shake of head, the melancholy smile,
The sigh almost a sob! What's wrong, was right erewhile?
Why are we two at once such ocean-width apart?
Pale fingers press my arm, and sad eyes probe my heart.

Why is the wife in trouble?

This way, this way, Fifine!
Here 's she, shall make my thoughts be surer what they mean!
First let me read the signs, portray you past mistake
The gypsy's foreign self, no swarth our sun could bake.
Yet where 's a woolly trace degrades the wiry hair?
And note the Greek-nymph nose, and—oh, my Hebrew pair
Of eye and eye—o'erarched by velvet of the mole—
That swim as in a sea, that dip and rise and roll,
Spilling the light around! While either ear is cut
Thin as a dusk-leaved rose carved from a cocoanut.
And then, her neck! now, grant you had the power to deck,
Just as your fancy pleased, the bistre-length of neck,
Could lay, to shine against its shade, a moonlike row
Of pearls, each round and white as bubble Cupids blow
Big out of mother's milk,—what pearl-moon would surpass
That string of mock-turquoise, those almandines of glass,
Where girlhood terminates? for with breasts'-birth commence
The boy, and page-costume, till pink and impudence
End admirably all: complete the creature trips
Our way now, brings sunshine upon her spangled hips,
As here she fronts us full, with pose half-frank, half-fierce!

Words urged in vain, Elvire! You waste your quart and tierce,
Lunge at a phantom here, try fence in fairy-land.
For me, I own defeat, ask but to understand
The acknowledged victory of whom I call my queen,
Sexless and bloodless sprite: though mischievous and mean,
Yet free and flower-like too, with loveliness for law,
And self-sustainment made morality.

A flaw
Do you account i' the lily, of lands which travellers know,
That, just as golden gloom supersedes Northern snow
I' the chalice, so, about each pistil, spice is packed,—
Deliriously-drugged scent, in lieu of odor lacked,
With us, by bee and moth, their banquet to enhance
At morn and eve, when dew, the chilly sustenance,

Needs mixture of some chaste and temperate perfume?
I ask, is she in fault who guards such golden gloom,
Such dear and damning scent, by who cares what devices,
And takes the idle life of insects she entices
When, drowned to heart's desire, they satiate the inside
O' the lily, mark her wealth and manifest her pride?

XVIII

But, wiser, we keep off, nor tempt the acrid juice;
Discreet we peer and praise, put rich things to right use.
No flavorous venomed bell,—the rose it is, I wot,
Only the rose, we pluck and place, unwronged a jot,
No worse for homage done by every devotee,
I' the proper loyal throne, on breast where rose should be.
Or if the simpler sweets we have to choose among,
Would taste between our teeth, and give its toy the tongue,—
O gorgeous poison-plague, on thee no hearts are set!
We gather daisy meek, or maiden violet:
I think it is Elvire we love, and not Fifine.

XIX

"How does she make my thoughts be sure of what they mean?"
Judge and be just! Suppose, an age and time long past
nenew for our behoof one pageant more, the last
O' the kind, sick Louis liked to see defile between
Him and the yawning grave, its passage served to screen.
With eye as gray as lead, with cheek as brown as bronze,
Here where we stand, shall sit and suffer Louis Onze:
The while from yonder tent parade forth, not—oh, no—
Bateleurs, baladines! but range themselves a-row
Those well-sung women-worthies whereof loud fame still finds
Some echo linger faint, less in our hearts than minds.

XX

See, Helen! pushed in front o' the world's worst night and storm,
By Lady Venus' hand on shoulder: the sweet form
Shrinkingly prominent, though mighty, like a moon
Outbreaking from a cloud, to put harsh things in tune,
And magically bring mankind to acquiesce
In its own ravage,—call no curse upon, but bless
(Beldame, a moment since) the outbreaking beauty, now,
That casts o'er all the blood a candor from her brow.

See, Cleopatra! bared, the entire and sinuous wealth
O' the shining shape; each orb of indolent ripe health,
Captured, just where it finds a fellow-orb as fine
I' the body: traced about by jewels which outline,
Fire-frame, and keep distinct, perfections—lest they melt
To soft smooth unity ere half their hold be felt:
Yet, o'er that white and wonder, a soul's predominance
I' the head so high and haught—except one thievish glance,
From back of oblong eye, intent to count the slain.
Hush,—oh, I know, Elvire! Be patient, more remain!
What say you to Saint? ... Pish! Whatever Saint you please,
Cold-pinnacled aloft o' the spire, prays calm the seas
From Pornic Church, and oft at midnight (peasants say)
Goes walking out to save from shipwreck: well she may!
For think how many a year has she been conversant
With naught but winds and rains, sharp courtesy and scant
O' the wintry snow that coats the pent-house of her shrine,
Covers each knee, climbs near, but spares the smile benign
Which seems to say, "I looked for scarce so much from earth!"
She follows, one long thin pure finger in the girth
O' the girdle—whence the folds of garment, eye and eye,
Besprent with fleurs-de-lys, flow down and multiply
Around her feet,—and one, pressed hushingly to lip:
As if, while thus we made her march, some foundering ship
Might miss her from her post, nearer to God halfway
In heaven, and she inquired, "Who that treads earth can pray?
I doubt if even she, the unashamed! though, sure,
She must have stripped herself only to clothe the poor."

XXI

This time, enough 's a feast, not one more form, Elvire!
Provided you allow that, bringing up the rear
O' the bevy I am loth to—by one bird—curtail,
First note may lead to last, an octave crown the scale,
And this feminity be followed—do not flout!—
By—who concludes the masque with curtsey, smile and pout,
Submissive-mutinous? No other than Fifine
Points toe, imposes haunch, and pleads with tambourine!

XXII

"Well, what 's the meaning here, what does the masque intend,
Which, unabridged, we saw file past us, with no end
Of fair ones, till Fifine came, closed the catalogue?"

XXIII

Task fancy yet again! Suppose you cast this clog
Of flesh away (that weeps, upbraids, withstands my arm)
And pass to join your peers, paragon charm with charm,
As I shall show you may,—prove best of beauty there!
Yourself confront yourself! This, help me to declare
That yonder-you, who stand beside these, braving each
And blinking none, beat her who lured to Troy-town beach
The purple prows of Greece,—nay, beat Fifine; whose face,
Mark how I will inflame, when seigneur-like I place
I' the tambourine, to spot the strained and piteous blank
Of pleading parchment, see, no less than a whole franc!

XXIV

Ah, do you mark the brown o' the cloud, made bright with fire
Through and through? as, old wiles succeeding to desire,
Quality (you and I) once more compassionate
A hapless infant, doomed (fie on such partial fate!)
To sink the inborn shame, waive privilege of sex,
And posture as you see, support the nods and becks
Of clowns that have their stare, nor always pay its price;
An infant born perchance as sensitive and nice
As any soul of you, proud dames, whom destiny
Keeps uncontaminate from stigma of the sty
She wallows in! You draw back skirts from filth like her
Who, possibly, braves scorn, if, scorned, she minister
To age, want, and disease of parents one or both;
Nay, peradventure, stoops to degradation, loth
That some just-budding sister, the dew yet on the rose,
Should have to share in turn the ignoble trade,—who knows?

XXV

Ay, who indeed! Myself know nothing, but dare guess
That oft she trips in haste to hand the booty ... yes,
'Twixt fold and fold of tent, there looms he, dim-discerned,
The ogre, lord of all those lavish limbs have earned!
—Brute-beast-face,—ravage, sear, scowl and malignancy,—
O' the Strong Man, whom (no doubt, her husband) by and by
You shall behold do feats: lift up nor quail beneath
A quintal in each hand, a cart-wheel 'twixt his teeth.
Oh, she prefers sheer strength to ineffective grace,
Breeding and culture! seeks the essential in the case!

To him has flown my franc; and welcome, if that squint
O' the diabolic eye so soften through absinthe,
That for once, tambourine, tunic and tricot 'scape
Their customary curse "Not half the gain o' the ape!"
Ay, they go in together!

XXVI

Yet still her phantom stays
Opposite, where you stand: as steady 'neath our gaze,—
The live Elvire's and mine,—though fancy stuff and mere
Illusion; to be judged—dream-figures—without fear
Or favor, those the false, by you and me the true.

XXVII

"What puts it in my head to make yourself judge you?"
Well, it may be, the name of Helen brought to mind
A certain myth I mused in years long left behind:
How she that fled from Greece with Paris whom she loved,
And came to Troy, and there found shelter, and so proved
Such cause of the world's woe,—how she, old stories call
This creature, Helen's self, never saw Troy at all.
Jove had his fancy-fit, must needs take empty air,
Fashion her likeness forth, and set the phantom there
I' the midst for sport, to try conclusions with the blind
And blundering race, the game create for Gods, mankind:
Experiment on these,—establish who would yearn
To give up life for her, who, other-minded, spurn
The best her eyes could smile,—make half the world sublime,
And half absurd, for just a phantom all the time!
Meanwhile true Helen's self sat, safe and far away,
By a great river-side, beneath a purer day,
With solitude around, tranquillity within;
Was able to lean forth, look, listen, through the din
And stir; could estimate the worthlessness or worth
Of Helen who inspired such passion to the earth,
A phantom all the time! That put it in my head
To make yourself judge you—the phantom-wife instead
O' the tearful true Elvire!

XXVIII

I thank the smile at last
Which thins away the tear! Our sky was overcast,

And something fell; but day clears up: if there chanced rain,
The landscape glistens more. I have not vexed in vain
Elvire: because she knows, now she has stood the test,
How, this and this being good, herself may still be best
O' the beauty in review; because the flesh that claimed
Unduly my regard, she thought, the taste, she blamed
In me, for things externe, was all mistake, she finds,—
Or will find, when I prove that bodies show me minds,
That, through the outward sign, the inward grace allures,
And sparks from heaven transpierce earth's coarsest covertures,
All by demonstrating-the value of Fifine!

XXIX

Partake my confidence! No creature 's made so mean
But that, some way, it boasts, could we investigate,
Its supreme worth: fulfils, by ordinance of fate,
Its momentary task, gets glory all its own,
Tastes triumph in the world, pre-eminent, alone.
Where is the single grain of sand, 'mid millions heaped.
Confusedly on the beach, but, did we know, has leaped
Or will leap, would we wait, i' the century, some once,
To the very throne of things?—earth's brightest for the nonce,
When sunshine shall impinge on just that grain's facette
Which fronts him fullest, first, returns his ray with jet
Of promptest praise, thanks God best in creation's name!
As firm is my belief, quick sense perceives the same
Self-vindicating flash illustrate every man
And woman of our mass, and prove, throughout the plan,
No detail but, in place allotted it, was prime
And perfect.

XXX

Witness her, kept waiting all this time!
What happy angle makes Fifine reverberate
Sunshine, least sand-grain, she, of shadiest social state?
No adamantine shield, polished like Helen there,
Fit to absorb the sun, regorge him till the glare,
Dazing the universe, draw Troy-ward those blind beaks
Of equal-sided ships rowed by the well-greaved Greeks!
No Asian mirror, like yon Ptolemaic witch
Able to fix sun fast and tame sun down, enrich,
Not burn the world with beams thus flatteringly rolled
About her, head to foot, turned slavish snakes of gold!
And oh, no tinted pane of oriel sanctity,

Does our Fifine afford, such as permits supply
Of lustrous heaven, revealed, far more than mundane sight
Could master, to thy cell, pure Saint! where, else too bright,
So suits thy sense the orb, that, what outside was noon,
Pales, through thy lozenged blue, to meek benefic moon!
What then? does that prevent each dunghill, we may pass
Daily, from boasting too its bit of looking-glass,
Its sherd which, sun-smit, shines, shoots arrowy fire beyond
That satin-muffled mope, your sulky diamond?

XXXI

And now, the mingled ray she shoots, I decompose.
Her antecedents, take for execrable! Gloze
No whit on your premiss: let be, there was no worst
Of degradation spared Fifine: ordained from first
To last, in body and soul, for one life-long debauch,
The Pariah of the North, the European Nautch!
This, far from seek to hide, she puts in evidence
Calmly, displays the brand, bids pry without offence
Your finger on the place. You comment, "Fancy us
So operated on, maltreated, mangled thus!
Such torture in our case, had we survived an hour?
Some other sort of flesh and blood must be, with power
Appropriate to the vile, unsensitive, tough-thonged,
In lieu of our fine nerve! Be sure, she was not wronged
Too much: you must not think she winced at prick as we!"
Come, come, that 's what you say, or would, were thoughts but free.

XXXII

Well then, thus much confessed, what wonder if there steal
Unchallenged to nay heart the force of one appeal
She makes, and justice stamp the sole claim she asserts?
So absolutely good is truth, truth never hurts
The teller, whose worst crime gets somehow grace, avowed.
To me, that silent pose and prayer proclaimed aloud:
"Know all of me outside, the rest be emptiness
For such as you! I call attention to my dress,
Coiffure, outlandish features, lithe memorable limbs,
Piquant entreaty, all that eye-glance overskims.
Does this give pleasure? Then, repay the pleasure, put
Its price i' the tambourine! Do you seek further? Tut!
I 'm just my instrument,—sound hollow: mere smooth skin
Stretched o'er gilt framework, I; rub-dub, naught else within—
Always, for such as you! — if I have use elsewhere,

If certain bells, now mute, can jingle, need you care?
Be it enough, there 's truth i' the pleading, which comports
With no word spoken out in cottages or courts,
Since all I plead is, 'Pay for just the sight you see,
And give no credit to another charm in me!'
Do I say, like your Love? 'To praise my face is well,
But, who would know my worth, must search my heart to tell!'
Do I say, like your Wife? 'Had I passed in review
The produce of the globe, my man of men were—you!'
Do I say, like your Helen? 'Yield yourself up, obey
Implicitly, nor pause to question, to survey
Even the worshipful! prostrate you at my shrine!
Shall you dare controvert what the world counts divine?
Array your private taste, own liking of the sense,
Own longing of the soul, against the impudence
Of history, the blare and bullying of verse?
As if man ever yet saw reason to disburse
The amount of what sense liked, soul longed for,—given, devised
As love, forsooth,—until the price was recognized
As moderate enough by divers fellow-men!
Then, with his warrant safe that these would love too, then,
Sure that particular gain implies a public loss,
And that no smile he buys but proves a slash across
The face, a stab into the side of somebody—
Sure that, along with love's main-purchase, he will buy
Up the whole stock of earth's uncharitableness,
Envy and hatred,—then, decides he to profess
His estimate of one, by love discerned, though dim
To all the world beside: since what 's the world to him?'
Do I say, like your Queen of Egypt? 'Who foregoes
My cup of witchcraft—fault be on the fool! He knows
Nothing of how I pack my wine-press, turn its winch
Three-times-three, all the time to song and dance, nor flinch
From charming on and on, till at the last I squeeze
Out the exhaustive drop that leaves behind mere lees
And dregs, vapidity, thought essence heretofore!
Sup of my sorcery, old pleasures please no more!
Be great, be good, love, learn, have potency of hand
Or heart or head,—what boots? You die, nor understand
What bliss might be in life: you ate the grapes, but knew
Never the taste of wine, such vintage as I brew!'
Do I say, like your Saint? 'An exquisitest touch
Bides in the birth of things: no after-time can much
Enhance that fine, that faint, fugitive first of all!
What color paints the cup o' the May-rose, like the small
Suspicion of a blush which doubtfully begins?
What sound outwarbles brook, while, at the source, it wins
That moss and stone dispart, allow its bubblings breathe?

What taste excels the fruit, just where sharp flavors sheathe
Their sting, and let encroach the honey that allays?
And so with soul and sense; when sanctity betrays
First fear lest earth below seem real as heaven above,
And holy worship, late, change soon to sinful love—
Where is the plenitude of passion which endures
Comparison with that, I ask of amateurs?'
Do I say, like Elvire" ...

(Your husband holds you fast,
Will have you listen, learn your character at last!)
"Do I say?—like her mixed unrest and discontent,
Reproachfulness and scorn, with that submission blent
So strangely, in the face, by sad smiles and gay tears,—
Quiescence which attacks, rebellion which endears,—
Say? 'As you loved me once, could you but love me now!
Years probably have graved their passage on my brow,
Lips turn more rarely red, eyes sparkle less than erst;
Such tribute body pays to time; but, unamerced,
The soul retains, nay, boasts old treasure multiplied.
Though dew-prime flee,—mature at noonday, love defied
Chance, the wind, change, the rain: love strenuous all the more
For storm, struck deeper root and choicer fruitage bore,
Despite the rocking world; yet truth struck root in vain:
While tenderness bears fruit, you praise, not taste again.
Why? They are yours, which once were hardly yours, might go
To grace another's ground: and then—the hopes we know,
The fears we keep in mind!—when, ours to arbitrate,
Your part was to bow neck, bid fall decree of fate.
Then, O the knotty point—white-night's work to revolve—
What meant that smile, that sigh? Not Solon's self could solve!
Then, O the deep surmise what one word might express,
And if what seemed her "No" may not have meant her "Yes!"
Then, such annoy, for cause—calm welcome, such acquist
Of rapture if, refused her arm, hand touched her wrist!
Now, what 's a smile to you? Poor candle that lights up
The decent household gloom which sends you out to sup.
A tear? worse! warns that health requires you keep aloof
From nuptial chamber, since rain penetrates the roof!
Soul, body got and gained, inalienably safe
Your own, become despised; more worth has any waif
Or stray from neighbor's pale: pouch that,—'t is pleasure, pride,
Novelty, property, and larceny beside!
Preposterous thought! to find no value fixed in things,
To covet all you see, hear, dream of, till fate brings

About that, what you want, you gain; then follows change.
Give you the sun to keep, forthwith must fancy range:
A goodly lamp, no doubt,—yet might you catch her hair
And capture, as she frisks, the fen-fire dancing there!
What do I say? at least a meteor 's half in heaven;
Provided filth but shine, my husband hankers even
After putridity that 's phosphorescent, cribs
The rustic's tallow-rush, makes spoil of urchins' squibs,
In short, prefers to me—chaste, temperate, serene—
What sputters green and blue, this fizgig called Fifine!'"

XXXIV

So all your sex mistake! Strange that so plain a fact
Should raise such dire debate! Few families were racked
By torture self-supplied, did Nature grant but this—
That women comprehend mental analysis!

XXXV

Elvire, do you recall when, years ago, our home
The intimation reached, a certain pride of Rome,
Authenticated piece, in the third, last and best
Manner—whatever, fools and connoisseurs contest,—
No particle disturbed by rude restorer's touch,
The palaced picture-pearl, so long eluding clutch
Of creditor, at last, the Rafael might—could we
But come to terms—change lord, pass from the Prince to me?
I think you recollect my fever of a year:
How the Prince would, and how he would not; now,—too dear
That promise was, he made his grandsire so long since,
Rather to boast "I own a Rafael" than "am Prince!"
And now, the fancy soothed—if really sell he must
His birthright for a mess of pottage—such a thrust
I' the vitals of the Prince were mollified by balm,
Could he prevail upon his stomach to bear qualm,
And bequeath Liberty (because a purchaser
Was ready with the sum—a trifle!) yes, transfer
His heart at all events to that land where, at least,
Free institutions reign! And so, its price increased
Fivefold (Americans are such importunates!),
Soon must his Rafael start for the United States.
Oh, alternating bursts of hope now, then despair!
At last, the bargain 's struck, I 'm all but beggared, there
The Rafael faces me, in fine, no dream at all,
My housemate, evermore to glorify my wall.

A week must pass, before heart-palpitations sink,
In gloating o'er my gain, so late I edged the brink
Of doom; a fortnight more, I spend in Paradise:
"Was outline e'er so true, could coloring entice
So calm, did harmony and quiet so avail?
How right, how resolute, the action tells the tale!"
A month, I bid my friends congratulate their best:
"You happy Don!" (to me): "The blockhead!" (to the rest):
"No doubt he thinks his daub original, poor dupe!"
Then I resume my life: one chamber must not coop
Man's life in, though it boast a marvel like my prize.
Next year, I saunter past with unaverted eyes,
Nay, loll and turn my back: perchance to overlook
With relish, leaf by leaf, Doré's last picture-book.

XXXVI

Imagine that a voice reproached me from its frame:
"Here do I hang, and may! Your Rafael, just the same,
'T is only you that change; no ecstasies of yore!
No purposed suicide distracts you any more!"
Prompt would my answer meet such frivolous attack:
"You misappropriate sensations. What men lack,
And labor to obtain, is hoped and feared about
After a fashion; what they once obtain, makes doubt,
Expectancy's old fret and fume, henceforward void.
But do they think to hold such havings unalloyed
By novel hopes and fears, of fashion just as new,
To correspond i' the scale? Nowise, I promise you!
Mine you are, therefore mine will be, as fit to cheer
My soul and glad my sense to-day as this-day-year.
So, any sketch or scrap, pochade, caricature,
Made in a moment, meant a moment to endure,
I snap at, seize, enjoy, then tire of, throw aside,
Find you in your old place. But if a servant cried
'Fire in the gallery!'—methinks, were I engaged
In Doré, elbow-deep, picture-books million-paged
To the four winds would pack, sped by the heartiest curse
Was ever launched from lip, to strew the universe.
Would not I brave the best o' the burning, bear away
Either my perfect piece in safety, or else stay
And share its fate, be made its martyr, nor repine?
Inextricably wed, such ashes mixed with mine!"

XXXVII

For which I get the eye, the hand, the heart, the whole
O' the wondrous wife again!

XXXVIII

But no, play out your rôle
I' the pageant! 'T is not fit your phantom leave the stage:
I want you, there, to make you, here, confess you wage
Successful warfare, pique those proud ones, and advance
Claim to ... equality? nay, but predominance
In physique o'er them all, where Helen heads the scene
Closed by its tiniest of tail-tips, pert Fifine.
How ravishingly pure you stand in pale constraint!
My new-created shape, without or touch or taint,
Inviolate of life and worldliness and sin—
Fettered, I hold my flower, her own cup's weight would win
From off the tall slight stalk a-top of which she turns
And trembles, makes appeal to one who roughly earns
Her thanks instead of blame, (did lily only know,)
By thus constraining length of lily, letting snow
Of cup-crown, that 's her face, look from its guardian stake,
Superb on all that crawls beneath, and mutely make
Defiance, with the mouth's white movement of disdain,
To all that stoops, retires, and hovers round again!
How windingly the limbs delay to lead up, reach
Where, crowned, the head waits calm: as if reluctant, each,
That eye should traverse quick such lengths of loveliness,
From feet, which just are found embedded in the dress
Deep swathed about with folds and flowings virginal,
Up to the pleated breasts, rebellious 'neath their pall,
As if the vesture's snow were moulding sleep not death,
Must melt and so release; whereat, from the fine sheath,
The flower-cup-crown starts free, the face is unconcealed,
And what shall now divert me, once the sweet face revealed,
From all I loved so long, so lingeringly left?

XXXIX

Because indeed your face fits into just the cleft
O' the heart of me, Elvire, makes right and whole once more
All that was half itself without you! As before,
My truant finds its place! Doubtlessly sea-shells yearn,
If plundered by sad chance: would pray their pearls return,
Let negligently slip away into the wave!
Never may eyes desist, those eyes so gray and grave,
From their slow sure supply of the effluent soul within!

And, would you humor me? I dare to ask, unpin
The web of that brown hair! O'erwash o' the sudden, but
As promptly, too, disclose, on either side, the jut
Of alabaster brow! So part rich rillets dyed
Deep by the woodland leaf, when down they pour, each side
O' the rock-top, pushed by Spring!

XL

"And where i' the world is all
This wonder, you detail so trippingly, espied?
My mirror would reflect a tall, thin, pale, deep-eyed
Personage, pretty once, it may be, doubtless still
Loving,—a certain grace yet lingers, if you will,—
But all this wonder, where?"

XLI

Why, where but in the sense
And soul of me, Art's judge? Art is my evidence
That something was, is, might be; but no more thing itself,
Than flame is fuel. Once the verse-book laid on shelf,
The picture turned to wall, the music fled from ear,—
Each beauty, born of each, grows clearer and more clear,
Mine henceforth, ever mine!

XLII

But if I would retrace
Effect, in Art, to cause,—corroborate, erase
What 's right or wrong i' the lines, test fancy in my brain
By fact which gave it birth? I re-peruse in vain
The verse, I fail to find that vision of delight
I' the Bazzi's lost-profile, eye-edge so exquisite.
And, music: what? that burst of pillared cloud by day
And pillared fire by night, was product, must we say,
Of modulating just, by enharmonic change,—
The augmented sixth resolved,—from out the straighter range
Of D sharp minor—leap of disimprisoned thrall—
Into thy light and life, D major natural?

XLIII

Elvire, will you partake in what I shall impart?

I seem to understand the way heart chooses heart
By help of the outside form,—a reason for our wild
Diversity in choice,—why each grows reconciled
To what is absent, what superfluous in the mask
Of flesh that 's meant to yield,—did nature ply her task
As artist should,—precise the features of the soul,
Which, if in any case they found expression, whole
I' the traits, would give a type, undoubtedly display
A novel, true, distinct perfection in its way.
Never shall I believe any two souls were made
Similar; granting, then, each soul of every grade
Was meant to be itself, prove in itself complete,
And, in completion, good,—nay, best o' the kind,—as meet
Needs must it be that show on the outside correspond
With inward substance,—flesh, the dress which soul has donned,
Exactly reproduce,—were only justice done
Inside and outside too,—types perfect every one.
How happens it that here we meet a mystery
Insoluble to man, a plaguy puzzle? Why
Each soul is either made imperfect, and deserves
As rude a face to match; or else a bungler swerves,
And nature, on a soul worth rendering aright,
Works ill, or proves perverse, or, in her own despite,
—Here too much, there too little,—bids each face, more or less,
Retire from beauty, make approach to ugliness?
And yet succeeds the same: since, what is wanting to success,
If somehow every face, no matter how deform,
Evidence, to some one of hearts on earth, that, warm
Beneath the veriest ash, there hides a spark of soul
Which, quickened by love's breath, may yet pervade the whole
O' the gray, and, free again, be fire?—of worth the same,
Howe'er produced, for, great or little, flame is flame.
A mystery, whereof solution is to seek.

XLIV

I find it in the fact that each soul, just as weak
Its own way as its fellow,—departure from design
As flagrant in the flesh,—goes striving to combine
With what shall right the wrong, the under or above
The standard: supplement unloveliness by love.
—Ask Plato else! And this corroborates the sage,
That Art,—which I may style the love of loving, rage
Of knowing, seeing, feeling the absolute truth of things
For truth's sake, whole and sole, not any good, truth brings
The knower, seer, feeler, beside,—instinctive Art
Must fumble for the whole, once fixing on a part

However poor, surpass the fragment, and aspire
To reconstruct thereby the ultimate entire.
Art, working with a will, discards the superflux,
Contributes to defect, toils on till,—fiat lux,—
There 's the restored, the prime, the individual type!

XLV

Look, for example now! This piece of broken pipe
(Some shipman's solace erst) shall act as crayon; and
What tablet better serves my purpose than the sand?
—Smooth slab whereon I draw, no matter with what skill,
A face, and yet another, and yet another still.
There lie my three prime types of beauty!

XLVI

Laugh your best!
"Exaggeration and absurdity?" Confessed!
Yet, what may that face mean, no matter for its nose,
A yard long, or its chin, a foot short?

XLVII

"You suppose,
Horror?" Exactly! What 's the odds if, more or less
By yard or foot, the features do manage to express
Such meaning in the main? Were I of Gérôme's force,
Nor feeble as you see, quick should my crayon course
O'er outline, curb, excite, till,—so completion speeds
With Gérôme well at work,—observe how brow recedes,
Head shudders back on spine, as if one haled the hair,
Would have the full-face front what pin-point eye's sharp stare
Announces; mouth agape to drink the flowing fate,
While chin protrudes to meet the burst o' the wave: elate
Almost, spurred on to brave necessity, expend
All life left, in one flash, as fire does at its end.
Retrenchment and addition effect a masterpiece,
Not change i' the motive: here dimmish, there increase—
And who wants Horror, has it.

XLVIII

Who wants some other show

Of soul, may seek elsewhere—this second of the row?
What does it give for germ, monadic mere intent
Of mind in face, faint first of meanings ever meant?
Why, possibly, a grin, that, strengthened, grows a laugh;
That, softened, leaves a smile; that, tempered, bids you quaff
At such a magic cup as English Reynolds once
Compounded: for the witch pulls out of you response
Like Garrick's to Thalia, however due may be
Your homage claimed by that stiff-stoled Melpomene!

XLIX

And just this one face more! Pardon the bold pretence!
May there not lurk some hint, struggle toward evidence
In that compressed mouth, those strained nostrils, steadfast eyes
Of utter passion, absolute self-sacrifice,
Which—could I but subdue the wild grotesque, refine
That bulge of brow, make blunt that nose's aquiline,
And let, although compressed, a point of pulp appear
I' the mouth—would give at last the portrait of Elvire?

L

Well, and if so succeed hand-practice on awry
Preposterous art-mistake, shall soul-proficiency
Despair,—when exercised on nature, which at worst
Always implies success,—however crossed and curst
By failure,—such as art would emulate in vain?
Shall any soul despair of setting free again
Trait after trait, until the type as wholly start
Forth, visible to sense, as that minutest part,
(Whate'er the chance,) which first arresting eye, warned soul
That, under wrong enough and ravage, lay the whole
O' the loveliness it "loved"—I take the accepted phrase?

LI

So I account for tastes: each chooses, none gainsays
The fancy of his fellow, a paradise for him,
A hell for all beside. You can but crown the brim
O' the cup; if it be full, what matters less or more?
Let each, i' the world, amend his love, as I, o' the shore,
My sketch, and the result as undisputed be!
Their handiwork to them, and my Elvire to me:
—Result more beautiful than beauty's self, when lo,

What was my Rafael turns my Michelagnolo!

LII

For, we two boast, beside our pearl, a diamond.
I' the palace-gallery, the corridor beyond,
Upheaves itself a marble, a magnitude man-shaped
As snow might be. One hand—the Master's—smoothed and scraped
That mass, he hammered on and hewed at, till he hurled
Life out of death, and left a challenge: for the world,
Death still,—since who shall dare, close to the image, say
If this be purposed Art, or mere mimetic play
Of Nature?—wont to deal with crag or cloud, as stuff
To fashion novel forms, like forms we know, enough
For recognition, but enough unlike the same,
To leave no hope ourselves may profit by her game;
Death therefore to the world. Step back a pace or two!
And then, who dares dispute the gradual birth its due
Of breathing life, or breathless immortality,
Where out she stands, and yet stops short, half bold, half shy,
Hesitates on the threshold of things, since partly blent
With stuff she needs must quit, her native element
I' the mind o' the Master,—what 's the creature, dear-divine
Yet earthly-awful too, so manly-feminine,
Pretends this white advance? What startling brain-escape
Of Michelagnolo takes elemental shape?
I think he meant the daughter of the old man o' the sea,
Emerging from her wave, goddess Eidotheé—
She who, in elvish sport, spite with benevolence
Mixed Mab-wise up, must needs instruct the Hero whence
Salvation dawns o'er that mad misery of his isle.
Yes, she imparts to him, by what a pranksome wile
He may surprise her sire, asleep beneath a rock,
When he has told their tale, amid his webfoot flock
Of sea-beasts, "fine fat seals with bitter breath!" laughs she
At whom she likes to save, no less: Eidotheé,
Whom you shall never face evolved, in earth, in air,
In wave; but, manifest i' the soul's domain, why, there
She ravishingly moves to meet you, all through aid
O' the soul! Bid shine what should, dismiss into the shade
What should not be,—and there triumphs the paramount
Emprise o' the Master! But, attempt to make account
Of what the sense, without soul's help perceives? I bought
That work—(despite plain proof, whose hand it was had wrought
I' the rough: I think we trace the tool of triple tooth,
Here, there, and everywhere)—bought dearly that uncouth
Unwieldy bulk, for just ten dollars—"Bulk, would fetch—

Converted into lime—some five pauls!" grinned a wretch,
Who, bound on business, paused to hear the bargaining,
And would have pitied me "but for the fun o' the thing!"

LIII

Shall such a wretch be—you? Must—while I show Elvire
Shaming all other forms, seen as I see her here
I' the soul,—this other-you perversely look outside,
And ask me, "Where i' the world is charm to be descried
I' the tall thin personage, with paled eye, pensive face,
Any amount of love, and some remains of grace?"
See yourself in my soul!

LIV

And what a world for each
Must somehow be i' the soul,—accept that mode of speech,—
Whether an aura gird the soul, wherein it seems
To float and move, a belt of all the glints and gleams
It struck from out that world, its weaklier fellows found
So dead and cold; or whether these not so much surround,
As pass into the soul itself, add worth to worth,
As wine enriches blood, and straightway send it forth,
Conquering and to conquer, through all eternity,
That 's battle without end.

LV

I search but cannot see
What purpose serves the soul that strives, or world it tries
Conclusions with, unless the fruit of victories
Stay, one and all, stored up and guaranteed its own
Forever, by some mode whereby shall be made known
The gain of every life. Death reads the title clear—
What each soul for itself conquered from out things here:
Since, in the seeing soul, all worth lies, I assert,—
And naught i' the world, which, save for soul that sees, inert
Was, is, and would be ever,—stuff for transmuting,—null
And void until man's breath evoke the beautiful—
But, touched aright, prompt yields each particle its tongue
Of elemental flame,—no matter whence flame sprung
From gums and spice, or else from straw and rottenness,
So long as soul has power to make them burn, express
What lights and warms henceforth, leaves only ash behind,

Howe'er the chance: if soul be privileged to find
Food so soon that, by first snatch of eye, suck of breath,
It can absorb pure life: or, rather, meeting death
I' the shape of ugliness, by fortunate recoil
So put on its resource, it find therein a foil
For a new birth of life, the challenged soul's response
To ugliness and death,—creation for the nonce.

LVI

I gather heart through just such conquests of the soul,
Through evocation out of that which, on the whole,
Was rough, ungainly, partial accomplishment, at best,
And—what, at worst, save failure to spit at and detest?—
—Through transference of all, achieved in visible things,
To where, secured from wrong, rest soul's imaginings—
Through ardor to bring help just where completion halts,
Do justice to the purpose, ignore the slips and faults—
And, last, through waging with deformity a fight
Which wrings thence, at the end, precise its opposite.
I praise the loyalty o' the scholar,—stung by taunt
Of fools, "Does this evince thy Master men so vaunt?
Did he then perpetrate the plain abortion here?"—
Who cries, "His work am I! full fraught by him, I clear
His fame from each result of accident and time,
Myself restore his work to its fresh morning-prime,
Not daring touch the mass of marble, fools deride,
But putting my idea in plaster by its side,
His, since mine; I, he made, vindicate who made me!"

LVII

For you must know, I too achieved Eidotheé,
In silence and by night—dared justify the lines
Plain to my soul, although, to sense, that triple-tine's
Achievement halt halfway, break down, or leave a blank.
If she stood forth at last, the Master was to thank!
Yet may there not have smiled approval in his eyes—
That one at least was left who, born to recognize
Perfection in the piece imperfect, worked, that night,
In silence, such his faith, until the apposite
Design was out of him, truth palpable once more?
And then—for at one blow, its fragments strewed the floor—
Recalled the same to live within his soul as heretofore.

LVIII

And, even as I hold and have Eidotheé,
I say, I cannot think that gain,—which would not be
Except a special soul had gained it,—that such gain
Can ever be estranged, do aught but appertain
Immortally, by right firm, indefeasible,
To who performed the feat, through God's grace and man's will!
Gain, never shared by those who practised with earth's stuff,
And spoiled whate'er they touched, leaving its roughness rough,
Its blankness bare, and, when the ugliness opposed,
Either struck work or laughed "He doted or he dozed!"

LIX

While, oh, how all the more will love become intense
Hereafter, when "to love" means yearning to dispense,
Each soul, its own amount of gain through its own mode
Of practising with life, upon some soul which owed
Its treasure, all diverse and yet in worth the same,
To new work and changed way! Things furnish you rose-flame,
Which burn up red, green, blue, nay, yellow more than needs,
For me, I nowise doubt; why doubt a time succeeds
When each one may impart, and each receive, both share
The chemic secret, learn,—where I lit force, why there
You drew forth lambent pity,—where I found only food
For self-indulgence, you still blew a spark at brood
I' the grayest ember, stopped not till self-sacrifice imbued
Heaven's face with flame? What joy, when each may supplement
The other, changing each, as changed, till, wholly blent,
Our old things shall be new, and, what we both ignite,
Fuse, lose the varicolor in achromatic white!
Exemplifying law, apparent even now
In the eternal progress,—love's law, which I avow
And thus would formulate: each soul lives, longs and works
For itself, by itself, because a lodestar lurks,
An other than itself,—in whatsoe'er the niche
Of mistiest heaven it hide, whoe'er the Glumdalclich
May grasp the Gulliver: or it, or he, or she—
Theosutos e broteios eper kekramene,—
(For fun's sake, where the phrase has fastened, leave it fixed!
So soft it says,—"God, man, or both together mixed!")
This, guessed at through the flesh, by parts which prove the whole,
This constitutes the soul discernible by soul
—Elvire, by me!

"And then"—(pray you, permit remain
This hand upon my arm!—your cheek dried, if you deign,
Choosing my shoulder)—"then!"—(Stand up for, boldly state
The objection in its length and breadth!) "You abdicate,
With boast yet on your lip, soul's empire, and accept
The rule of sense; the Man, from monarch's throne has stept—
Leapt, rather, at one bound, to base, and there lies, Brute.
You talk of soul,—how soul, in search of soul to suit,
Must needs review the sex, the army, rank and file
Of womankind, report no face nor form so vile
But that a certain worth, by certain signs, may thence
Evolve itself and stand confessed—to soul—by sense.
Sense? Oh, the loyal bee endeavors for the hive!
Disinterested hunts the flower-field through, alive
Not one mean moment, no,—suppose on flower he light,—
To his peculiar drop, petal-dew perquisite,
Matter-of-course snatched snack: unless he taste, how try?
This, light on tongue-tip laid, allows him pack his thigh,
Transport all he counts prize, provision for the comb,
Food for the future day,—a banquet, but at home!
Soul? Ere you reach Fifine's, some flesh may be to pass!
That bombéd brow, that eye, a kindling chrysopras,
Beneath its stiff black lash, inquisitive how speeds
Each functionary limb, how play of foot succeeds,
And how you let escape or duly sympathize
With gastro-knemian grace,—true, your soul tastes and tries,
And trifles time with these, but, fear not, will arrive
At essence in the core, bring honey home to hive,
Brain-stock and heart-stuff both—to strike objectors dumb—
Since only soul affords the soul fit pabulum!
Be frank for charity! Who is it you deceive—
Yourself or me or God, with all this make-believe?"

And frank I will respond as you interrogate.
Ah, Music, wouldst thou help! Words struggle with the weight
So feebly of the False, thick element between
Our soul, the True, and Truth! which, but that intervene
False shows of things, were reached as easily by thought
Reducible to word, as now by yearnings wrought
Up with thy fine free force, O Music, that canst thrid,
Electrically win a passage through the lid
Of earthly sepulchre, our words may push against,
Hardly transpierce as thou! Not dissipate, thou deign'st,

So much as tricksily elude what words attempt
To heave away, i' the mass, and let the soul, exempt
From all that vapory obstruction, view, instead
Of glimmer underneath, a glory overhead.
Not feebly, like our phrase, against the barrier go
In suspirative swell the authentic notes I know,
By help whereof, I would our souls were found without
The pale, above the dense and dim which breeds the doubt!
But Music, dumb for you, withdraws her help from me;
And, since to weary words recourse again must be,
At least permit they rest their burden here and there,
Music-like: cover space! My answer,—need you care
If it exceed the bounds, reply to questioning
You never meant should plague? Once fairly on the wing,
Let me flap far and wide!

LXII

For this is just the time,
The place, the mood in you and me, when all things chime.
Clash forth life's common chord, whence, list how there ascend
Harmonics far and faint, till our perception end,—
Reverberated notes whence we construct the scale
Embracing what we know and feel and are! How fail
To find or, better, lose your question, in this quick
Reply which nature yields, ample and catholic?
For, arm in arm, we too have reached, nay, passed, you see,
The village-precinct; sun sets mild on Sainte-Marie—
We only catch the spire, and yet I seem to know
What 's hid i' the turn o' the hill: how all the graves must glow
Soberly, as each warms its little iron cross,
Flourished about with gold, and graced (if private loss
Be fresh) with stiff rope-wreath of yellow crisp bead-blooms
Which tempt down birds to pay their supper, 'mid the tombs,
With prattle good as song, amuse the dead awhile,
If couched they hear beneath the matted camomile!

LXIII

Bid them good-by before last friend has sung and supped!
Because we pick our path and need our eyes,—abrupt
Descent enough,—but here 's the beach, and there 's the bay,
And, opposite, the streak of Île Noirmoutier.
Thither the waters tend; they freshen as they haste,
At feel o' the night-wind, though, by cliff and cliff embraced,
This breadth of blue retains its self-possession still;

As you and I intend to do, who take our fill
Of sights and sounds—soft sound, the countless hum and skip
Of insects we disturb, and that good fellowship
Of rabbits our footfall sends huddling, each to hide
He best knows how and where; and what whirred past, wings wide?
That was, an owl, their young may justlier apprehend!
Though you refuse to speak, your beating heart, my friend,
I feel against my arm,—though your bent head forbids
A look into your eyes, yet, on my cheek, their lids
That ope and shut, soft send a silken thrill the same.
Well, out of all and each these nothings, comes—what came
Often enough before, the something that would aim
Once more at the old mark: the impulse to at last
Succeed where hitherto was failure in the past,
And yet again essay the adventure. Clearlier sings
No bird to its couched corpse, "Into the truth of things—
Out of their falseness rise, and reach thou, and remain!

LXIV

"That rise into the true out of the false—explain?"
May an example serve? In yonder bay I bathed,
This sunny morning: swam my best, then hung, half swathed
With chill, and half with warmth, i' the channel's midmost deep:
You know how one—not treads, but stands in water? Keep
Body and limbs below, hold head back, uplift chin,
And, for the rest, leave care! If brow, eyes, mouth, should win
Their freedom,—excellent! If they must brook the surge,
No matter though they sink, let but the nose emerge.
So, all of me in brine lay soaking: did I care
One jot? I kept alive by man's due breath of air
I' the nostrils, high and dry. At times, o'er these would run
The ripple, even wash the wavelet,—morning's sun
Tempted advance, no doubt: and always flash of froth,
Fish-outbreak, bubbling by, would find me nothing loth
To rise and look around; then all was overswept
With dark and death at once. But trust the old adept!
Back went again the head, a merest motion made,
Fin-fashion, either hand, and nostril soon conveyed
Assurance light and life were still in reach as erst:
Always the last and—wait and watch—sometimes the first.
Try to ascend breast-high? wave arms wide free of tether?
Be in the air and leave the water altogether?
Under went all again, till I resigned myself
To only breathe the air, that 's footed by an elf,
And only swim the water, that 's native to a fish.
But there is no denying that, ere I curbed my wish,

And schooled my restive arms, salt entered mouth and eyes
Often enough—sun, sky, and air so tantalize!
Still, the adept swims, this accorded, that denied;
Can always breathe, sometimes see and be satisfied!

LXV

I liken to this play o' the body—fruitless strife
To slip the sea and hold the heaven—my spirit's life
'Twixt false, whence it would break, and true, where it would bide.
I move in, yet resist, am upborne every side
By what I beat against, an element too gross
To live in, did not soul duly obtain her dose
Of life-breath, and inhale from truth's pure plenitude
Above her, snatch and gain enough to just illude
With hope that some brave bound may baffle evermore
The obstructing medium, make who swam henceforward soar:
—Gain scarcely snatched when, foiled by the very effort, souse,
Underneath ducks the soul, her truthward yearnings dowse
Deeper in falsehood! ay, but fitted less and less
To bear in nose and mouth old briny bitterness
Proved alien more and more: since each experience proves
Air—the essential good, not sea, wherein who moves
Must thence, in the act, escape, apart from will or wish.
Move a mere hand to take water-weed, jelly-fish,
Upward you tend! And yet our business with the sea
Is not with air, but just o' the water, watery:
We must endure the false, no particle of which
Do we acquaint us with, but up we mount a pitch
Above it, find our head reach truth, while hands explore
The false below: so much while here we bathe,—no more!

LXVI

Now, there is one prime point (hear and be edified!)
One truth more true for me than any truth beside—
To-wit, that I am I, who have the power to swim,
The skill to understand the law whereby each limb
May bear to keep immersed, since, in return, made sure
That its mere movement lifts head clean through coverture.
By practice with the false, I reach the true? Why, thence
It follows, that the more I gain self-confidence,
Get proof I know the trick, can float, sink, rise, at will,
The better I submit to what I have the skill
To conquer in my turn, even now, and by and by
Leave wholly for the land, and there laugh, shake me dry

To last drop, saturate with noonday—no need more
Of wet and fret, plagued once: on Pornic's placid shore,
Abundant air to breathe, sufficient sun to feel!
Meantime I buoy myself: no whit my senses reel
When over me there breaks a billow; nor, elate
Too much by some brief taste, I quaff intemperate
The air, o'ertop breast-high the wave-environment.
Full well I know the thing I grasp, as if intent
To hold,—my wandering wave,—will not be grasped at all:
The solid-seeming grasped, the handful great or small
Must go to nothing, glide through fingers fast enough;
But none the less, to treat liquidity as stuff—
Though failure—certainly succeeds beyond its aim,
Sends head above, past thing that hands miss, or the same.

LXVII

So with this wash o' the world, wherein lifelong we drift;
We push and paddle through the foam by making shift
To breathe above at whiles when, after deepest duck
Down underneath the show, we put forth hand and pluck
At what seems somehow like reality—a soul.
I catch at this and that, to capture and control,
Presume I hold a prize, discover that my pains
Are run to naught: my hands are balked, my head regains
The surface where I breathe and look about, a space.
The soul that helped me mount? Swallowed up in the race
O' the tide, come who knows whence, gone gayly who knows where!
I thought the prize was mine; I flattered myself there.
It did its duty, though: I felt it, it felt me;
Or, where I look about and breathe, I should not be.
The main point is—the false fluidity was bound
Acknowledge that it frothed o'er substance, nowise found
Fluid, but firm and true. Man, outcast, "howls,"—at rods?—
If "sent in playful spray a-shivering to his gods!"
Childishest childe, man makes thereby no bad exchange.
Stay with the flat-fish, thou! We like the upper range
Where the "gods" live, perchance the dæmons also dwell:
Where operates a Power, which every throb and swell
Of human heart invites that human soul approach,
"Sent" near and nearer still, however "spray" encroach
On "shivering" flesh below, to altitudes, which gained,
Evil proves good, wrong right, obscurity explained,
And "howling" childishness. Whose howl have we to thank.
If all the dogs 'gan bark and puppies whine, till sank
Each yelper's tail 'twixt legs? for Huntsman Common-sense
Came to the rescue, bade prompt thwack of thong dispense

Quiet i' the kennel; taught that ocean might be blue,
And rolling and much more, and yet the soul have, too,
Its touch of God's own flame, which he may so expand,
"Who measurèd the waters i' the hollow of his hand,"
That ocean's self shall dry, turn dewdrop in respect
Of all-triumphant fire, matter with intellect
Once fairly matched; bade him who egged on hounds to bay,
Go curse, i' the poultry yard, his kind: "there let him lay"
The swan's one addled egg: which yet shall put to use,
Rub breast-bone warm against, so many a sterile goose!

LXVIII

No, I want sky not sea, prefer the larks to shrimps,
And never dive so deep but that I get a glimpse
O' the blue above, a breath of the air around. Elvire,
I seize—by catching at the melted beryl here,
The tawny hair that just has trickled off,—Fifine!
Did not we two trip forth to just enjoy the scene,
The tumbling-troop arrayed, the strollers on their stage,
Drawn up and under arms, and ready to engage—
Dabble, and there an end, with foam and froth o'er face,
Till suddenly Fifine suggested change of place?
Now we taste æther, scorn the ware, and interchange apace
No ordinary thoughts, but such as evidence
The cultivated mind in both. On what pretence
Are you and I to sneer at who lent help to hand,
And gave the lucky lift?

LXIX

Still sour? I understand!
One ugly circumstance discredits my fair plan—
That Woman does the work: I waive the help of Man.
"Why should experiment be tried with only waves,
When solid spars float round? Still some Thalassia saves
Too pertinaciously, as though no Triton, bluff
As e'er blew brine from conch, were free to help enough!
Surely, to recognize a man, his mates serve best!
Why is there not the same or greater interest
In the strong spouse as in the pretty partner, pray,
Were recognition just your object, as you say,
Amid this element o' the false?"

LXX

We come to terms.
I need to be proved true; and nothing so confirms
One's faith in the prime point that one 's alive, not dead,
In all Descents to Hell whereof I ever read,
As when a phantom there, male enemy or friend,
Or merely stranger-shade, is struck, is forced suspend
His passage: "You that breathe, along with us the ghosts?"
Here, why must it be still a woman that accosts?

LXXI

Because, one woman 's worth, in that respect, such hairy hosts
Of the other sex and sort! Men? Say you have the power
To make them yours, rule men, throughout life's little hour,
According to the phrase; what follows? Men, you make,
By ruling them, your own: each man for his own sake
Accepts you as his guide, avails him of what worth
He apprehends in you to sublimate his earth
With fire: content, if so you convoy him through night,
That you shall play the sun, and he, the satellite,
Pilfer your light and heat and virtue, starry pelf,
While, caught up by your course, he turns upon himself.
Women rush into you, and there remain absorbed.
Beside, 't is only men completely formed, full-orbed,
Are fit to follow track, keep pace, illustrate so
The leader: any sort of woman may bestow
Her atom on the star, or clod she counts for such,—
Each little making less bigger by just that much.
Women grow you, while men depend on you at best.
And what dependence! Bring and put him to the test,
Your specimen disciple, a handbreadth separate
From you, he almost seemed to touch before! Abate
Complacency you will, I judge, at what 's divulged!
Some flabbiness you fixed, some vacancy out-bulged,
Some—much—nay, all, perhaps, the outward man 's your work:
But, inside man?—find him, wherever he may lurk,
And where 's a touch of you in his true self?

LXXII

I wish
Some wind would waft this way a glassy bubble-fish
O' the kind the sea inflates, and show you, once detached
From wave ... or no, the event is better told than watched:
Still may the thing float free, globose and opaline

All over, save where just the amethysts combine
To blue their best, rim-round the sea-flower with a tinge
Earth's violet never knew! Well, 'neath that gem-tipped fringe,
A head lurks—of a kind—that acts as stomach too;
Then comes the emptiness which out the water blew
So big and belly-like, but, dry of water drained,
Withers away nine-tenths. Ah, but a tenth remained!
That was the creature's self: no more akin to sea,
Poor rudimental head and stomach, you agree,
Than sea 's akin to sun who yonder dips his edge.

LXXIII

But take the rill which ends a race o'er yonder ledge
O' the fissured cliff, to find its fate in smoke below!
Disengage that, and ask—what news of life, you know
It led, that long lone way, through pasture, plain and waste?
All 's gone to give the sea! no touch of earth, no taste
Of air, reserved to tell how rushes used to bring
The butterfly and bee, and fisher-bird that 's king
O' the purple kind, about the snow-soft silver-sweet
Infant of mist and dew; only these atoms fleet,
Embittered evermore, to make the sea one drop
More big thereby—if thought keep count where sense must stop.

LXXIV

The full-blown ingrate, mere recipient of the brine,
That takes all and gives naught, is Man; the feminine
Rillet that, taking all and giving naught in turn,
Goes headlong to her death i' the sea, without concern
For the old inland life, snow-soft and silver-clear,
That 's woman—typified from Fifine to Elvire.

LXXV

Then, how diverse the modes prescribed to who would deal
With either kind of creature! 'T is Man, you seek to seal
Your very own? Resolve, for first step, to discard
Nine-tenths of what you are! To make, you must be marred,—
To raise your race, must stoop,—to teach them aught, must learn
Ignorance, meet halfway what most you hope to spurn
I' the sequel. Change yourself, dissimulate the thought
And vulgarize the word, and see the deed be brought
To look like nothing done with any such intent

As teach men—though perchance it teach, by accident!
So may you master men: assured that if you show
One point of mastery, departure from the low
And level,—head or heart-revolt at long disguise,
Immurement, stifling soul in mediocrities,—
If inadvertently a gesture, much more, word
Reveal the hunter no companion for the herd,
His chance of capture 's gone. Success means, they may snuff,
Examine, and report,—a brother, sure enough,
Disports him in brute-guise; for skin is truly skin,
Horns, hoofs, are hoofs and horns, and all, outside and in,
Is veritable beast, whom fellow-beasts resigned
May follow, made a prize in honest pride, behind
One of themselves and not creation's upstart lord!
Well, there 's your prize i' the pound—much joy may it afford
My Indian! Make survey and tell me,—was it worth
You acted part so well, went all-fours upon earth
The live-long day, brayed, belled, and all to bring to pass
That stags should deign eat hay when winter stints them grass?

LXXVI

So much for men, and how disguise may make them mind
Their master. But you have to deal with womankind?
Abandon stratagem for strategy! Cast quite
The vile disguise away, try truth clean-opposite
Such creep-and-crawl, stand forth all man and, might it chance,
Somewhat of angel too!—whate'er inheritance,
Actual on earth, in heaven prospective, be your boast,
Lay claim to! Your best self revealed at uttermost,—
That 's the wise way o' the strong! And e'en should falsehood tempt
The weaker sort to swerve,—at least the lie 's exempt
From slur, that 's loathlier still, of aiming to debase
Rather than elevate its object. Mimic grace,
Not make deformity your mask! Be sick by stealth,
Nor traffic with disease—malingering in health!
No more of: "Countrymen, I boast me one like you—
My lot, the common strength, the common weakness too!
I think the thoughts you think; and if I have the knack
Of fitting thoughts to words, you peradventure lack,
Envy me not the chance, yourselves more fortunate!
Many the loaded ship self-sunk through treasure freight,
Many the pregnant brain brought never child to birth,
Many the great heart broke beneath its girdle-girth!
Be mine the privilege to supplement defect,
Give dumbness voice, and let the laboring intellect
Find utterance in word, or possibly in deed!

What though I seem to go before? 't is you that lead!
I follow what I see so plain—the general mind
Projected pillar-wise, flame kindled by the kind,
Which dwarfs the unit—me—to insignificance!
Halt you, I stop forthwith,—proceed, I too advance!"

Ay, that 's the way to take with men you wish to lead,
Instruct and benefit. Small prospect you succeed
With women so! Be all that 's great and good and wise,
August, sublime—swell out your frog the right ox-size—
He 's buoyed like a balloon, to soar, not burst, you 'll see!
The more you prove yourself, less fear the prize will flee
The captor. Here you start after no pompous stag
Who condescends be snared, with toss of horn, and brag
Of bray, and ramp of hoof; you have not to subdue
The foe through letting him imagine he snares you!
'T is rather with ...

Ah, thanks! quick—where the dipping disk
Shows red against the rise and fall o' the fin! there frisk
In shoal the—porpoises? Dolphins, they shall and must
Cut through the freshening clear—dolphins, my instance just!
'T is fable, therefore truth: who has to do with these,
Needs never practice trick of going hands and knees
As beasts require. Art fain the fish to captivate?
Gather thy greatness round, Arion! Stand in state,
As when the banqueting thrilled conscious—like a rose
Throughout its hundred leaves at that approach it knows
Of music in the bird—while Corinth grew one breast
A-throb for song and thee; nay, Periander pressed
The Methymnæan hand, and felt a king indeed, and guessed
How Phœbus' self might give that great mouth of the gods
Such a magnificence of song! The pillar nods,
Rocks roof, and trembles door, gigantic, post and jamb,
As harp and voice rend air—the shattering dithyramb!
So stand thou, and assume the robe that tingles yet
With triumph; strike the harp, whose every golden fret
Still smoulders with the flame, was late at fingers' end—
So, standing on the bench o' the ship, let voice expend
Thy soul, sing, unalloyed by meaner mode, thine own,
The Orthian lay; then leap from music's lofty throne
Into the lowest surge, make fearlessly thy launch!

Whatever storm may threat, some dolphin will be stanch!
Whatever roughness rage, some exquisite sea-thing
Will surely rise to save, will bear—palpitating—
One proud humility of love beneath its load—
Stem tide, part wave, till both roll on, thy jewell'd road
Of triumph, and the grim o' the gulf grow wonder-white
I' the phosphorescent wake; and still the exquisite
Sea-thing stems on, saves still, palpitatingly thus,
Lands safe at length its load of love at Tænarus,
True woman-creature!

LXXIX

Man? Ah, would you prove what power
Marks man,—what fruit his tree may yield, beyond the sour
And stinted crab, he calls love-apple, which remains
After you toil and moil your utmost,—all, love gains
By lavishing manure?—try quite the other plan!
And, to obtain the strong true product of a man,
Set him to hate a little! Leave cherishing his root,
And rather prune his branch, nip off the pettiest shoot
Superfluous on his bough! I promise, you shall learn
By what grace came the goat, of all beasts else, to earn
Such favor with the god o' the grape: 't was only he
Who, browsing on its tops, first stung fertility
Into the stock's heart, stayed much growth of tendril-twine,
Some faintish flower, perhaps, but gained the indignant wine,
Wrath of the red press! Catch the puniest of the kind—
Man-animalcule, starved body, stunted mind,
And, as you nip the blotch 'twixt thumb and finger-nail,
Admire how heaven above and earth below avail
No jot to soothe the mite, sore at God's prime offence
In making mites at all,—coax from its impotence
One virile drop of thought, or word, or deed, by strain
To propagate for once—which nature rendered vain,
Who lets first failure stay, yet cares not to record
Mistake that seems to cast opprobrium on the Lord!
Such were the gain from love's best pains! But let the elf
Be touched with hate, because some real man bears himself
Manlike in body and soul, and, since he lives, must thwart
And furify and set a-fizz this counterpart
O' the pismire that 's surprised to effervescence, if,
By chance, black bottle come in contact with chalk cliff,
Acid with alkali! Then thrice the bulk, out blows
Our insect, does its kind, and cuckoo-spits some rose!

No—'t is ungainly work, the ruling men, at best!
The graceful instinct 's right: 't is women stand confessed
Auxiliary, the gain that never goes away,
Takes nothing and gives all: Elvire, Fifine, 't is they
Convince,—if little, much, no matter!—one degree
The more, at least, convince unreasonable me
That I am, anyhow, a truth, though all else seem
And be not: if I dream, at least I know I dream.
The falsity, beside, is fleeting: I can stand
Still, and let truth come back,—your steadying touch of hand
Assists me to remain self-centred, fixed amid
All on the move. Believe in me, at once you bid
Myself believe that, since one soul has disengaged
Mine from the shows of things, so much is fact: I waged
No foolish warfare, then, with shades, myself a shade,
Here in the world—may hope my pains will be repaid!
How false things are, I judge: how changeable, I learn:
When, where, and how it is I shall see truth return,
That I expect to know, because Fifine knows me!—
How much more, if Elvire!

"And why not, only she?
Since there can be for each, one Best, no more, such Best,
For body and mind of him, abolishes the rest
O' the simply Good and Better. You please select Elvire
To give you this belief in truth, dispel the fear
Yourself are, after all, as false as what surrounds;
And why not be content? When we two watched the rounds
The boatman made, 'twixt shoal and sandbank, yesterday,
As, at dead slack of tide, he chose to push his way,
With oar and pole, across the creek, and reach the isle
After a world of pains—my word provoked your smile,
Yet none the less deserved reply: "T were wiser wait
The turn o' the tide, and find conveyance for his freight—
How easily—within the ship to purpose moored,
Managed by sails, not oars! But no,—the man 's allured
By liking for the new and hard in his exploit!
First come shall serve! He makes—courageous and adroit—
The merest willow-leaf of boat do duty, bear
His merchandise across: once over, needs he care
If folk arrive by ship, six hours hence, fresh and gay?'
No: he scorns commonplace, affects the unusual way;
And good Elvire is moored, with not a breath to flap

The yards of her, no lift of ripple to o'erlap
Keel, much less, prow. What care? since here 's a cockle-shell,
Fifine, that 's taut and crank, and carries just as well
Such seamanship as yours!"

Alack, our life is lent,
From first to last, the whole, for this experiment
Of proving what I say—that we ourselves are true!
I would there were one voyage, and then no more to do
But tread the firm-land, tempt the uncertain sea no more
I would we might dispense with change of shore for shore
To evidence our skill, demonstrate—in no dream
It was, we tided o'er the trouble of the stream.
I would the steady voyage, and not the fitful trip,—
Elvire, and not Fifine,—might test our seamanship.
But why expend one's breath to tell you, change of boat
Means change of tactics too? Come see the same afloat
To-morrow, all the change, new stowage fore and aft
O' the cargo; then, to cross requires new sailor-craft!
To-day, one step from stern to bow keeps boat in trim:
To-morrow, some big stone—or woe to boat and him!—
Must ballast both. That man stands for Mind, paramount
Throughout the adventure: ay, howe'er you make account,
'T is mind that navigates,—skips over, twists between
The bales i' the boat,—now gives importance to the mean,
And now abates the pride of life, accepts all fact,
Discards all fiction,—steers Fifine, and cries, i' the act,
"Thou art so bad, and yet so delicate a brown!
Wouldst tell no end of lies: I talk to smile or frown!
Wouldst rob me: do men blame a squirrel, lithe and sly,
For pilfering the nut she adds to hoard? Nor I."
Elvire is true, as truth, honesty's self, alack!
The worse! too safe the ship, the transport there and back
Too certain! one may loll and lounge and leave the helm,
Let wind and tide do work: no fear that waves o'erwhelm
The steady-going bark, as sure to feel her way
Blindfold across, reach land, next year as yesterday!
How can I but suspect, the true feat were to slip
Down side, transfer myself to cockle-shell from ship,
And try if, trusting to sea-tracklessness, I class
With those around whose breast grew oak and triple brass:
Who dreaded no degree of death, but, with dry eyes,
Surveyed the turgid main and its monstrosities—
And rendered futile so, the prudent Power's decree
Of separate earth and disassociating sea;

Since, how is it observed, if impious vessels leap
Across, and tempt a thing they should not touch—the deep?
(See Horace to the boat, wherein, for Athens bound,
When Virgil must embark—Jove keep him safe and sound!—
The poet bade his friend start on the watery road,
Much reassured by this so comfortable ode.)

LXXXIII

Then, never grudge my poor Fifine her compliment!
The rakish craft could slip her moorings in the tent,
And, hoisting every stitch of spangled canvas, steer
Through divers rocks and shoals,—in fine, deposit here
Your Virgil of a spouse, in Attica: yea, thrid
The mob of men, select the special virtue hid
In him, forsooth, and say—or rather, smile so sweet,
"Of all the multitude, you—I prefer to cheat!
Are you for Athens bound? I can perform the trip,
Shove little pinnace off, while yon superior ship,
The Elvire, refits in port!" So, off we push from beach
Of Pornic town, and lo, ere eye can wink, we reach
The Long Walls, and I prove that Athens is no dream,
For there the temples rise! they are, they nowise seem!
Earth is not all one lie, this truth attests me true!
Thanks therefore to Fifine! Elvire, I 'm back with you!
Share in the memories! Embark I trust we shall
Together some fine day, and so, for good and all,
Bid Pornic Town adieu,—then, just the strait to cross,
And we reach harbor, safe, in Iostephanos!

LXXXIV

How quickly night comes! Lo, already 't is the land
Turns sea-like; overcrept by gray, the plains expand,
Assume significance; while ocean dwindles, shrinks
Into a pettier bound: its plash and plaint, methinks,
Six steps away, how both retire, as if their part
Were played, another force were free to prove her art,
Protagonist in turn! Are you unterrified?
All false, all fleeting too! And nowhere things abide,
And everywhere we strain that things should stay,—the one
Truth, that ourselves are true!

LXXXV

A word, and I have done.
Is it not just our hate of falsehood, fleetingness,
And the mere part, things play, that constitutes express
The inmost charm of this Fifine and all her tribe?
Actors! We also act, but only they inscribe
Their style and title so, and preface, only they,
Performance with "A lie is all we do or say."
Wherein but there can be the attraction, Falsehood's bribe,
That wins so surely o'er to Fifine and her tribe
The liking, nay the love of who hate Falsehood most,
Except that these alone of mankind make their boast
"Frankly, we simulate!" To feign, means—to have grace
And so get gratitude! This ruler of the race,
Crowned, sceptred, stoled to suit,—'t is not that you detect
The cobbler in the king, but that he makes effect
By seeming the reverse of what you know to be
The man, the mind, whole form, fashion, and quality.
Mistake his false for true, one minute,—there 's an end
Of the admiration! Truth, we grieve at or rejoice:
'T is only falsehood, plain in gesture, look and voice,
That brings the praise desired, since profit comes thereby.
The histrionic truth is in the natural lie.
Because the man who wept the tears was, all the time,
Happy enough; because the other man, a-grime
With guilt was, at the least, as white as I and you;
Because the timid type of bashful maidhood, who
Starts at her own pure shade, already numbers seven
Born babes and, in a month, will turn their odd to even;
Because the saucy prince would prove, could you unfurl
Some yards of wrap, a meek and meritorious girl—
Precisely as you see success attained by each
O' the mimes, do you approve, not foolishly impeach
The falsehood!

LXXXVI

That 's the first o' the truths found: all things, slow
Or quick i' the passage, come at last to that, you know!
Each has a false outside, whereby a truth is forced
To issue from within: truth, falsehood, are divorced
By the excepted eye, at the rare season, for
The happy moment. Life means—learning to abhor
The false, and love the true, truth treasured snatch by snatch,
Waifs counted at their worth. And when with strays they match
I' the particolored world,—when, under foul, shines fair,
And truth, displayed i' the point, flashes forth everywhere
I' the circle, manifest to soul, though hid from sense,

And no obstruction more affects this confidence,—
When faith is ripe for sight,—why, reasonably, then
Comes the great clearing-up. Wait threescore years and ten!

Therefore I prize stage-play, the honest cheating; thence
The impulse pricked, when fife and drum bade Fair commence,
To bid you trip and skip, link arm in arm with me,
Like husband and like wife, and so together see
The tumbling-troop arrayed, the strollers on their stage
Drawn up and under arms, and ready to engage.
And if I started thence upon abstruser themes ...
Well, 't was a dream, pricked too!

A poet never dreams:
We prose-folk always do: we miss the proper duct
For thoughts on things unseen, which stagnate and obstruct
The system, therefore; mind, sound in a body sane,
Keeps thoughts apart from facts, and to one flowing vein
Confines its sense of that which is not, but might be,
And leaves the rest alone. What ghosts do poets see?
What demons fear? what man or thing misapprehend?
Unchecked, the channel 's flush, the fancy 's free to spend
Its special self aright in manner, time and place.
Never believe that who create the busy race
O' the brain, bring poetry to birth, such act performed,
Feel trouble them, the same, such residue as warmed
My prosy blood, this morn,—intrusive fancies, meant
For outbreak and escape by quite another vent!
Whence follows that, asleep, my dreamings oft exceed
The bound. But you shall hear.

I smoked. The webs o' the weed,
With many a break i' the mesh, were floating to re-form
Cupola-wise above: chased thither by soft warm
Inflow of air without; since I—of mind to muse, to clench
The gain of soul and body, got by their noonday drench
In sun and sea—had flung both frames o' the window wide,
To soak my body still and let soul soar beside.
In came the country sounds and sights and smells—that fine

Sharp needle in the nose from our fermenting wine!
In came a dragon-fly with whir and stir, then out,
Off and away: in came,—kept coming, rather,—pout
Succeeding smile, and take-away still close on give,—
One loose long creeper-branch, tremblingly sensitive
To risks, which blooms and leaves,—each leaf tongue-broad, each bloom
Midfinger-deep,—must run by prying in the room
Of one who loves and grasps and spoils and speculates.
All so far plain enough to sight and sense: but, weights,
Measures and numbers,—ah, could one apply such test
To other visitants that came at no request
Of who kept open house,—to fancies manifold
From this four-cornered world, the memories new and old,
The antenatal prime experience—what know I?—
The initiatory love preparing us to die—
Such were a crowd to count, a sight to see, a prize
To turn to profit, were but fleshly ears and eyes
Able to cope with those o' the spirit!

XC

Therefore,—since
Thought hankers after speech, while no speech may evince
Feeling like music,—mine, o'erburdened with each gift
From every visitant, at last resolved to shift
Its burden to the back of some musician dead
And gone, who feeling once what I feel now, instead
Of words, sought sounds, and saved forever, in the same,
Truth that escapes prose,—nay, puts poetry to shame.
I read the note, I strike the key, I bid record
The instrument,—thanks greet the veritable word!
And not in vain I urge: "O dead and gone away,
Assist who struggles yet, thy strength become my stay,
Thy record serve as well to register—I felt
And knew thus much of truth! With me, must knowledge melt
Into surmise and doubt and disbelief, unless
Thy music reassure—I gave no idle guess,
But gained a certitude, I yet may hardly keep!
What care? since round is piled a monumental heap
Of music that conserves the assurance, thou as well
Wast certain of the same! thou, master of the spell,
Mad'st moonbeams marble, didst record what other men
Feel only to forget!" Who was it helped me, then?
What master's work first came responsive to my call,
Found my eye, fixed my choice?

Why, Schumann's "Carnival"!
My choice chimed in, you see, exactly with the sounds
And sights of yestereve, when, going on my rounds,
Where both roads join the bridge, I heard across the dusk
Creak a slow caravan, and saw arrive the husk
O' the spice-nut, which peeled off this morning, and displayed,
'Twixt tree and tree, a tent whence the red pennon made
Its vivid reach for home and ocean-idleness—
And where, my heart surmised, at that same moment,—yes,—
Tugging her tricot on—yet tenderly, lest stitch
Announce the crack of doom, reveal disaster which
Our Pornic's modest stock of merceries in vain
Were ransacked to retrieve,—there, cautiously a-strain,
(My heart surmised) must crouch in that tent's corner, curved
Like Spring-month's russet moon, some girl by fate reserved
To give me once again the electric snap and spark
Which prove, when finger finds out finger in the dark
O' the world, there 's fire and life and truth there, link but hands
And pass the secret on. Lo, link by link, expands
The circle, lengthens out the chain, till one embrace
Of high with low is found uniting the whole race,
Not simply you and me and our Fifine, but all
The world: the Fair expands into the Carnival,
And Carnival again to ... ah, but that 's my dream!

I somehow played the piece: remarked on each old theme
I' the new dress; saw how food o' the soul, the stuff that 's made
To furnish man with thought and feeling, is purveyed
Substantially the same from age to age, with change
Of the outside only for successive feasters, Range
The banquet-room o' the world, from the dim farthest head
O' the table, to its foot, for you and me bespread,
This merry morn, we find sufficient fare, I trow.
But, novel? Scrape away the sauce; and taste, below,
The verity o' the viand,—you shall perceive there went
To board-head just the dish which other condiment
Makes palatable now: guests came, sat down, fell-to,
Rose up, wiped mouth, went way,—lived, died,—and never knew
That generations yet should, seeking sustenance,
Still find the selfsame fare, with somewhat to enhance
Its flavor, in the kind of cooking. As with hates
And loves and fears and hopes, so with what emulates
The same, expresses hates, loves, fears, and hopes in Art:

The forms, the themes—no one without its counterpart
Ages ago; no one but, mumbled the due time
I' the mouth of the eater, needs be cooked again in rhyme,
Dished up anew in paint, sauce-smothered fresh in sound,
To suit the wisdom-tooth, just cut, of the age, that 's found
With gums obtuse to gust and smack which relished so
The meat o' the meal folk made some fifty years ago.
But don't suppose the new was able to efface
The old without a struggle, a pang! The commonplace
Still clung about his heart, long after all the rest
O' the natural man, at eye and ear, was caught, confessed
The charm of change, although wry lip and wrinkled nose
Owned ancient virtue more conducive to repose
Than modern nothings roused to somethings by some shred
Of pungency, perchance garlic in amber's stead.
And so on, till one day, another age, by due
Rotation, pries, sniffs, smacks, discovers old is new,
And sauce, our sires pronounced insipid, proves again
Sole piquant, may resume its titillating reign—
With music, most of all the arts, since change is there
The law, and not the lapse: the precious means the rare,
And not the absolute in all good save surprise.
So I remarked upon our Schumann's victories
Over the commonplace, how faded phrase grew fine,
And palled perfection—piqued, up-startled by that brine,
His pickle—bit the mouth and burnt the tongue aright,
Beyond the merely good no longer exquisite:
Then took things as I found, and thanked without demur
The pretty piece—played through that movement, you prefer
Where dance and shuffle past,—he scolding while she pouts,
She canting while he calms,—in those eternal bouts
Of age, the dog—with youth, the cat—by rose-festoon
Tied teasingly enough—Columbine, Pantaloon:
She, toe-tips and staccato,—legato, shakes his poll
And shambles in pursuit, the senior. Fi la folle!
Lie to him! get his gold and pay its price! begin
Your trade betimes, nor wait till you 've wed Harlequin
And need, at the week's end, to play the duteous wife,
And swear you still love slaps and leapings more than life!
Pretty! I say.

XCIII

And so, I somehow-nohow played
The whole o' the pretty piece; and then ... whatever weighed
My eyes down, furled the films about my wits? suppose,
The morning-bath,—the sweet monotony of those

Three keys, flat, flat and flat, never a sharp at all,—
Or else the brain's fatigue, forced even here to fall
Into the same old track, and recognize the shift
From old to new, and back to old again, and,—swift
Or slow, no matter,—still the certainty of change,
Conviction we shall find the false, where'er we range,
In art no less than nature: or what if wrist were numb,
And over-tense the muscle, abductor of the thumb,
Taxed by those tenths' and twelfths' unconscionable stretch?
Howe'er it came to pass, I soon was far to fetch—
Gone off in company with Music!

XCIV

Whither bound
Except for Venice? She it was, by instinct found
Carnival-country proper, who far below the perch
Where I was pinnacled, showed, opposite, Mark's Church,
And, underneath, Mark's Square, with those two lines of street,
Procuratié-sides, each leading to my feet—
Since from above I gazed, however I got there.

XCV

And what I gazed upon was a prodigious Fair,
Concourse immense of men and women, crowned or casqued,
Turbaned or tiar'd, wreathed, plumed, hatted or wigged, but masked—
Always masked,—only, how? No face-shape, beast or bird,
Nay, fish and reptile even, but some one had preferred,
From out its frontispiece, feathered or scaled or curled,
To make the vizard whence himself should view the world,
And where the world believed himself was manifest.
Yet when you came to look, mixed up among the rest
More funnily by far, were masks to imitate
Humanity's mishap: the wrinkled brow, bald pate,
And rheumy eyes of Age, peak'd chin and parchment chap,
Were signs of day-work done, and wage-time near,—mishap
Merely; but, Age reduced to simple greed and guile,
Worn apathetic else as some smooth slab, ere-while
A clear-cut man-at-arms i' the pavement, till foot's tread
Effaced the sculpture, left the stone you saw instead,—
Was not that terrible beyond the mere uncouth?
Well, and perhaps the next revolting you was Youth,
Stark ignorance and crude conceit, half smirk, half stare
On that frank fool-face, gay beneath its head of hair
Which covers nothing.

XCVI

These, you are to understand,
Were the mere hard and sharp distinctions. On each hand,
I soon became aware, flocked the infinitude
Of passions, loves and hates, man pampers till his mood
Becomes himself, the whole sole face we name him by,
Nor want denotement else, if age or youth supply
The rest of him: old, young,—classed creature: in the main
A love, a hate, a hope, a fear, each soul astrain
Some one way through the flesh—the face, an evidence
O' the soul at work inside; and, all the more intense,
So much the more grotesque.

XCVII

"Why should each soul be tasked
Some one way, by one love or else one hate?" I asked.
When it occurred to me, from all these sights beneath
There rose not any sound: a crowd, yet dumb as death!

XCVIII

Soon I knew why. (Propose a riddle, and 't is solved
Forthwith—in dream!) They spoke; but, since on me devolved
To see, and understand by sight,—the vulgar speech
Might be dispensed with. "He who cannot see, must reach
As best he may the truth of men by help of words
They please to speak, must fare at will of who affords
The banquet,"—so I thought. "Who sees not, hears and so
Gets to believe; myself it is that, seeing, know,
And, knowing, can dispense with voice and vanity
Of speech. What hinders then, that, drawing closer, I
Put privilege to use, see and know better still
These simulacra, taste the profit of my skill,
Down in the midst?"

XCIX

And plumb I pitched into the square—
A groundling like the rest. What think you happened there?
Precise the contrary of what one would expect!
For,—whereas, so much more monstrosities deflect

From nature and the type, as you the more approach
Their precinct,—here, I found brutality encroach
Less on the human, lie the lightlier as I looked
The nearlier on these faces that seemed but now so crook'd
And clawed away from God's prime purpose. They diverged
A little from the type, but somehow rather urged
To pity than disgust: the prominent, before,
Now dwindled into mere distinctness, nothing more.
Still, at first sight, stood forth undoubtedly the fact
Some deviation was: in no one case there lacked
The certain sign and mark, say hint, say, trick of lip
Or twist of nose, that proved a fault in workmanship,
Change in the prime design, some hesitancy here
And there, which checked the man and let the beast appear;
But that was all.

C

All; yet enough to bid each tongue
Lie in abeyance still. They talked, themselves among,
Of themselves, to themselves: I saw the mouths at play,
The gesture that enforced, the eye that strove to say
The same thing as the voice, and seldom gained its point
—That this was so, I saw; but all seemed out of joint
I' the vocal medium 'twixt the world and me. I gained
Knowledge by notice, not by giving ear,—attained
To truth by what men seemed, not said: to me one glance
Was worth whole histories of noisy utterance,
—At least, to me in dream.

CI

And presently I found
That, just as ugliness had withered, so unwound
Itself, and perished off, repugnance to what wrong
Might linger yet i' the make of man. My will was strong
I' the matter; I could pick and choose, project my weight:
(Remember how we saw the boatman trim his freight!)
Determine to observe, or manage to escape,
Or make divergency assume another shape
By shift of point of sight in me the observer: thus
Corrected, added to, subtracted from,—discuss
Each variant quality, and brute-beast touch was turned
Into mankind's safeguard! Force, guile, were arms which earned
My praise, not blame at all: for we must learn to live,
Case-hardened at all points, not bare and sensitive,

But plated for defence, nay, furnished for attack,
With spikes at the due place, that neither front nor back
May suffer in that squeeze with nature, we find—life.
Are we not here to learn the good of peace through strife,
Of love through hate, and reach knowledge by ignorance?
Why, those are helps thereto, which late we eyed askance,
And nicknamed unaware! Just so, a sword we call
Superfluous, and cry out against, at festival:
Wear it in time of war, its clink and clatter grate
O' the ear to purpose then!

CII

I found, one must abate
One's scorn of the soul's casing, distinct from the soul's self—
Which is the centre-drop: whereas the pride in pelf,
The lust to seem the thing it cannot be, the greed
For praise, and all the rest seen outside,—these indeed
Are the hard polished cold crystal environment
Of those strange orbs unearthed i' the Druid temple, meant
For divination (so the learned please to think)
Wherein you may admire one dewdrop roll and wink,
All unaffected by—quite alien to—what sealed
And saved it long ago: though how it got congealed
I shall not give a guess, nor how, by power occult,
The solid surface-shield was outcome and result
Of simple dew at work to save itself amid
The unwatery force around; protected thus, dew slid
Safe through all opposites, impatient to absorb
Its spot of life, and last forever in the orb
We, now, from hand to hand pass with impunity.

CIII

And the delight wherewith I watch this crowd must be
Akin to that which crowns the chemist when he winds
Thread up and up, till clue be fairly clutched,—unbinds
The composite, ties fast the simple to its mate,
And, tracing each effect back to its cause, elate,
Constructs in fancy, from the fewest primitives,
The complex and complete, all diverse life, that lives
Not only in beast, bird, fish, reptile, insect, but
The very plants and earths and ores. Just so I glut
My hunger both to be and know the thing I am,
By contrast with the thing I am not; so, through sham
And outside, I arrive at inmost real, probe

And prove how the nude form obtained the checkered robe.

CIV

—Experience, I am glad to master soon or late,
Here, there, and everywhere i' the world, without debate!
Only, in Venice why? What reason for Mark's Square
Rather than Timbuctoo?

CV

And I became aware,
Scarcely the word escaped my lips, that swift ensued
In silence and by stealth, and yet with certitude,
A formidable change of the amphitheatre
Which held the Carnival; although the human stir
Continued just the same amid that shift of scene.

CVI

For as on edifice of cloud i' the gray and green
Of evening,—built about some glory of the west,
To barricade the sun's departure,—manifest,
He plays, pre-eminently gold, gilds vapor, crag and crest
Which bend in rapt suspense above the act and deed
They cluster round and keep their very own, nor heed
The world at watch; while we, breathlessly at the base
O' the castellated bulk, note momently the mace
Of night fall here, fall there, bring change with every blow,
Alike to sharpened shaft and broadened portico
I' the structure: heights and depths, beneath the leaden stress,
Crumble and melt and mix together, coalesce,
Re-form, but sadder still, subdued yet more and more
By every fresh defeat, till wearied eyes need pore
No longer on the dull impoverished decadence
Of all that pomp of pile in towering evidence
So lately:—

CVII

Even thus nor otherwise, meseemed
That if I fixed my gaze awhile on what I dreamed
Was Venice' Square, Mark's Church, the scheme was straight unschemed,
A subtle something had its way within the heart

Of each and every house I watched, with counterpart
Of tremor through the front and outward face, until
Mutation was at end; impassive and stock-still
Stood now the ancient house, grown—new, is scarce the phrase,
Since older, in a sense,—altered to ... what i' the ways,
Ourselves are wont to see, coerced by city, town,
Or village, anywhere i' the world, pace up or down
Europe! In all the maze, no single tenement
I saw, but I could claim acquaintance with.

CVIII

There went
Conviction to my soul, that what I took of late
For Venice was the world; its Carnival—the state
Of mankind, masquerade in life-long permanence
For all time, and no one particular feast-day. Whence
'T was easy to infer what meant my late disgust
At the brute-pageant, each grotesque of greed and lust
And idle hate, and love as impotent for good—
When from my pride of place I passed the interlude
In critical review; and what, the wonder that ensued
When, from such pinnacled pre-eminence, I found
Somehow the proper goal for wisdom was the ground
And not the sky,—so, slid sagaciously betimes
Down heaven's baluster-rope, to reach the mob of mimes
And mummers; whereby came discovery there was just
Enough and not too much of hate, love, greed and lust,
Could one discerningly but hold the balance, shift
The weight from scale to scale, do justice to the drift
Of nature, and explain the glories by the shames
Mixed up in man, one stuff miscalled by different names
According to what stage i' the process turned his rough,
Even as I gazed, to smooth—only get close enough!
—What was all this except the lesson of a life?

CIX

And—consequent upon the learning how from strife
Grew peace—from evil, good—came knowledge that, to get
Acquaintance with the way o' the world, we must nor fret
Nor fume, on altitudes of self-sufficiency,
But bid a frank farewell to what—we think—should be,
And, with as good a grace, welcome what is—we find.

CX

Is—for the hour, observe! Since something to my mind
Suggested soon the fancy, nay, certitude that change,
Never suspending touch, continued to derange
What architecture, we, walled up within the cirque
O' the world, consider fixed as fate, not fairy-work.
For those were temples, sure, which tremblingly grew blank
From bright, then broke afresh in triumph,—ah, but sank
As soon, for liquid change through artery and vein
O' the very marble wound its way! And first a stain
Would startle and offend amid the glory; next,
Spot swift succeeded spot, but found me less perplexed
By portents; then, as 't were, a sleepiness soft stole
Over the stately fane, and shadow sucked the whole
Façade into itself, made uniformly earth
What was a piece of heaven; till, lo, a second birth,
And the veil broke away because of something new
Inside, that pushed to gain an outlet, paused in view
At last, and proved a growth of stone or brick or wood
Which, alien to the aim o' the Builder, somehow stood
The test, could satisfy, if not the early race
For whom he built, at least our present populace,
Who must not bear the blame for what, blamed, proves mishap
Of the Artist: his work gone, another fills the gap,
Serves the prime purpose so. Undoubtedly there spreads
Building around, above, which makes men lift their heads
To look at, or look through, or look—for aught I care—
Over: if only up, it is, not down, they stare.
"Commercing with the skies," and not the pavement in the Square.

CXI

But are they only temples that subdivide, collapse,
And tower again, transformed? Academies, perhaps!
Domes where dwells Learning, seats of Science, bower and hall
Which house Philosophy—do these, too, rise and fall,
Based though foundations be on steadfast mother-earth,
With no chimeric claim to supermundane birth,
No boast that, dropped from cloud, they did not grow from ground?
Why, these fare worst of all! these vanish and are found
Nowhere, by who tasks eye some twice within his term
Of threescore years and ten, for tidings what each germ
Has burgeoned out into, whereof the promise stunned
His ear with such acclaim,—praise-payment to refund
The praisers, never doubt, some twice before they die
Whose days are long i' the land.

CXII

Alack, Philosophy!
Despite the chop and change, diminished or increased,
Patched-up and plastered-o'er, Religion stands at least
I' the temple-type. But thou? Here gape I, all agog
These thirty years, to learn how tadpole turns to frog;
And thrice at least have gazed with mild astonishment,
As, skyward up and up, some fire-new fabric sent
Its challenge to mankind, that, clustered underneath
To hear the word, they straight believe, ay, in the teeth
O' the Past, clap hands, and hail triumphant Truth's outbreak—
Tadpole-frog-theory propounded past mistake!
In vain! A something ails the edifice, it bends,
It bows, it buries ... Haste! cry "Heads below" to friends—
But have no fear they find, when smother shall subside,
Some substitution perk with unabated pride
I' the predecessor's place!

CXIII

No,—the one voice which failed
Never, the preachment's coign of vantage nothing ailed,—
That had the luck to lodge i' the house not made with hands!
And all it preached was this: "Truth builds upon the sands,
Though stationed on a rock: and so her work decays,
And so she builds afresh, with like result. Naught stays
But just the fact that Truth not only is, but fain
Would have men know she needs must be, by each so plain
Attempt to visibly inhabit where they dwell."
Her works are work, while she is she; that work does well
Which lasts mankind their lifetime through, and lets believe
One generation more, that, though sand run through sieve,
Yet earth now reached is rock, and what we moderns find
Erected here is Truth, who, 'stablished to her mind
I' the fulness of the days, will never change in show
More than in substance erst: men thought they knew; we know!

CXIV

Do you, my generation? Well, let the blocks prove mist
I' the main enclosure,—church and college, if they list,
Be something for a time, and everything anon,
And anything awhile, as fit is off or on,

Till they grow nothing, soon to reappear no less
As something,—shape reshaped, till out of shapelessness
Come shape again as sure! no doubt, or round or square
Or polygon its front, some building will be there,
Do duty in that nook o' the wall o' the world where once
The Architect saw fit precisely to ensconce
College or church, and bid such bulwark guard the line
O' the barrier round about, humanity's confine.

CXV

Leave watching change at work i' the greater scale, on these
The main supports, and turn to their interstices
Filled up by fabrics too, less costly and less rare,
Yet of importance, yet essential to the Fair
They help to circumscribe, instruct, and regulate!
See, where each booth-front boasts, in letters small or great,
Its speciality, proclaims its privilege to stop
A breach, beside the best!

CXVI

Here History keeps shop,
Tells how past deeds were done, so and not otherwise:
"Man! hold truth evermore! forget the early lies!"
There sits Morality, demure behind her stall,
Dealing out life and death: "This is the thing to call
Right, and this other, wrong; thus think, thus do, thus say,
Thus joy, thus suffer!—not to-day as yesterday—
Yesterday's doctrine dead, this only shall endure!
Obey its voice and live!"—enjoins the dame demure.
While Art gives flag to breeze, bids drum beat, trumpet blow,
Inviting eye and ear to yonder raree-show.
Up goes the canvas, hauled to height of pole. I think,
We know the way—long lost, late learned—to paint! A wink
Of eye, and lo, the pose! the statue on its plinth!
How could we moderns miss the heart o' the labyrinth
Perversely all these years, permit the Greek seclude
His secret till to-day? And here 's another feud
Now happily composed: inspect this quartet-score!
Got long past melody, no word has Music more
To say to mortal man! But is the bard to be
Behindhand? Here 's his book, and now perhaps you see
At length what poetry can do!

CXVII

Why, that 's stability
Itself, that change on change we sorrowfully saw
Creep o'er the prouder piles! We acquiesced in law
When the fine gold grew dim i' the temple, when the brass
Which pillared that so brave abode where Knowledge was,
Bowed and resigned the trust; but, bear all this caprice,
Harlequinade where swift to birth succeeds decease
Of hue at every turn o' the tinsel-flag which flames
While Art holds booth in Fair? Such glories chased by shames
Like these, distract beyond the solemn and august
Procedure to decay, evanishment in dust,
Of those marmoreal domes,—above vicissitude,
We used to hope!

CXVIII

"So, all is change, in fine," pursued
The preachment to a pause. When—"All is permanence!"
Returned a voice. Within? without? No matter whence
The explanation came: for, understand, I ought
To simply say—"I saw," each thing I say "I thought."
Since ever, as, unrolled, the strange scene-picture grew
Before me, sight flashed first, though mental comment too
Would follow in a trice, come hobblingly to halt.

CXIX

So, what did I see next but,—much as when the vault
I' the west,—wherein we watch the vapory, manifold
Transfiguration,—tired turns blaze to black,—behold,
Peak reconciled to base, dark ending feud with bright,
The multiform subsides, becomes the definite.
Contrasting life and strife, where battle they i' the blank
Severity of peace in death, for which we thank
One wind that conies to quell the concourse, drive at last
Things to a shape which suits the close of things, and cast
Palpably o'er vexed earth heaven's mantle of repose?

CXX

Just so, in Venice' Square, that things were at the close
Was signalled to my sense; for I perceived arrest
O' the change all round about. As if some impulse pressed

Each gently into each, what was distinctness, late,
Grew vague, and, line from line no longer separate,
No matter what its style, edifice ... shall I say,
Died into edifice? I find no simpler way
Of saying how, without or dash or shock or trace
Of violence, I found unity in the place
Of temple, tower,—nay, hall and house and hut,—one blank
Severity of peace in death; to which they sank
Resigned enough, till ... ah, conjecture, I beseech,
What special blank did they agree to, all and each?
What common shape was that wherein they mutely merged
Likes and dislikes of form, so plain before?

CXXI

I urged
Your step this way, prolonged our path of enterprise
To where we stand at last, in order that your eyes
Might see the very thing, and save my tongue describe
The Druid monument which fronts you. Could I bribe
Nature to come in aid, illustrate what I mean,
What wants there she should lend to solemnize the scene?

CXXII

How does it strike you, this construction gaunt and gray—
Sole object, these piled stones, that gleam unground-away
By twilight's hungry jaw, which champs fine all beside
I' the solitary waste we grope through? Oh, no guide
Need we to grope our way and reach the monstrous door
Of granite! Take my word, the deeper you explore
That caverned passage, filled with fancies to the brim,
The less will you approve the adventure! such a grim
Bar-sinister soon blocks abrupt your path, and ends
All with a cold dread shape,—shape whereon Learning spends
Labor, and leaves the test obscurer for the gloss,
While Ignorance reads right—recoiling from that Cross!
Whence came the mass and mass, strange quality of stone
Unquarried anywhere i' the region round? Unknown!
Just as unknown, how such enormity could be
Conveyed by land, or else transported over sea,
And laid in order, so, precisely each on each,
As you and I would build a grotto where the beach
Sheds shell—to last an hour: this building lasts from age
To age the same. But why?

Ask Learning! I engage
You get a prosy wherefore, shall help you to advance
In knowledge just as much as helps you Ignorance
Surmising, in the mouth of peasant-lad or lass,
"I heard my father say he understood it was
A building, people built as soon as earth was made
Almost, because they might forget (they were afraid)
Earth did not make itself, but came of Somebody.
They labored that their work might last, and show thereby
He stays, while we and earth, and all things come and go.
Come whence? Go whither? That, when come and gone, we know
Perhaps, but not while earth and all things need our best
Attention: we must wait and die to know the rest.
Ask, if that 's true, what use in setting up the pile?
To make one fear and hope: remind us, all the while
We come and go, outside there 's Somebody that stays;
A circumstance which ought to make us mind our ways,
Because,—whatever end we answer by this life,—
Next time, best chance must be for who, with toil and strife,
Manages now to live most like what he was meant
Become: since who succeeds so far, 't is evident,
Stands foremost on the file; who fails, has less to hope
From new promotion. That 's the rule—with even a rope
Of mushrooms, like this rope I dangle! those that grew
Greatest and roundest, all in life they had to do,
Gain a reward, a grace they never dreamed, I think;
Since, outside white as milk and inside black as ink,
They go to the Great House to make a dainty dish
For Don and Donna; while this basket-load, I wish
Well off my arm, it breaks,—no starveling of the heap
But had his share of dew, his proper length of sleep
I' the sunshine: yet, of all, the outcome is—this queer
Cribbed quantity of dwarfs which burden basket here
Till I reach home; 't is there that, having run their rigs,
They end their earthly race, are flung as food for pigs.
Any more use I see? Well, you must know, there lies
Something, the Curé says, that points to mysteries
Above our grasp: a huge stone pillar, once upright,
Now laid at length, half-lost—discreetly shunning sight
I' the bush and brier, because of stories in the air—
Hints what it signified, and why was stationed there,
Once on a time. In vain the Curé tasked his lungs—
Showed, in a preachment, how, at bottom of the rungs
O' the ladder, Jacob saw, where heavenly angels stept
Up and down, lay a stone which served him, while he slept,

For pillow; when he woke, he set the same upright
As pillar, and a-top poured oil: things requisite
To instruct posterity, there mounts from floor to roof,
A staircase, earth to heaven; and also put in proof,
When we have sealed the sky, we well may let alone
What raised us from the ground, and—paying to the stone
Proper respect, of course—take staff and go our way,
Leaving the Pagan night for Christian break of day.
'For,' preached he, 'what they dreamed, these Pagans, wide-awake
We Christians may behold. How strange, then, were mistake
Did anybody style the stone,—because of drop
Remaining there from oil which Jacob poured a-top,—
Itself the Gate of Heaven, itself the end, and not
The means thereto!' Thus preached the Curé and no jot
The more persuaded people but that, what once a thing
Meant and had right to mean, it still must mean. So cling
Folk somehow to the prime authoritative speech,
And so distrust report, it seems as they could reach
Far better the arch-word, whereon their fate depends.
Through rude charactery, than all the grace it lends,
That lettering of your scribes! who flourish pen apace
And ornament the text, they say—we say, efface.
Hence, when the earth began its life afresh in May,
And fruit-trees bloomed, and waves would wanton, and the bay
Ruffle its wealth of weed, and stranger-birds arrive,
And beasts take each a mate,—folk, too, found sensitive,
Surmised the old gray stone upright there, through such tracts
Of solitariness and silence, kept the facts
Entrusted it, could deal out doctrine, did it please:
No fresh and frothy draught, but liquor on the lees,
Strong, savage, and sincere: first bleedings from a vine
Whereof the product now do Curés so refine
To insipidity, that, when heart sinks, we strive
And strike from the old stone the old restorative.
'Which is?'—why, go and ask our grandames how they used
To dance around it, till the Curé disabused
Their ignorance, and bade the parish in a band
Lay flat the obtrusive thing that cumbered so the land!
And there, accordingly, in bush and brier it—'bides
Its time to rise again!' (so somebody derides,
That 's pert from Paris,) 'since, yon spire, you keep erect
Yonder, and pray beneath, is nothing, I suspect,
But just the symbol's self, expressed in slate for rock,
Art's smooth for Nature's rough, new chip from the old block!'
There, sir, my say is said! Thanks, and Saint Gille increase
The wealth bestowed so well!"—wherewith he pockets piece,
Doffs cap, and takes the road. I leave in Learning's clutch
More money for his book, but scarcely gain as much.

To this it was, this same primeval monument,
That, in my dream, I saw building with building blent
Fall: each on each they fast and founderingly went
Confusion-ward; but thence again subsided fast,
Became the mound you see. Magnificently massed
Indeed, those mammoth-stones, piled by the Protoplast
Temple-wise in my dream! beyond compare with fanes
Which, solid-looking late, had left no least remains
I' the bald and blank, now sole usurper of the plains
Of heaven, diversified and beautiful before.
And yet simplicity appeared to speak no more
Nor less to me than spoke the compound. At the core,
One and no other word, as in the crust of late,
Whispered, which, audible through the transition-state,
Was no loud utterance in even the ultimate
Disposure. For as some imperial chord subsists,
Steadily underlies the accidental mists
Of music springing thence, that run their mazy race
Around, and sink, absorbed, back to the triad base,—
So, out of that one word, each variant rose and fell
And left the same "All 's change, but permanence as well."
—Grave note whence—list aloft!—harmonics sound, that mean:
"Truth inside, and outside, truth also; and between
Each, falsehood that is change, as truth is permanence.
The individual soul works through the shows of sense
(Which, ever proving false, still promise to be true)
Up to an outer soul as individual too;
And, through the fleeting, lives to die into the fixed,
And reach at length 'God, man, or both together mixed,'
Transparent through the flesh, by parts which prove a whole,
By hints which make the soul discernible by soul—
Let only soul look up, not down, not hate but love,
As truth successively takes shape, one grade above
Its last presentment, tempts as it were truth indeed
Revealed this time; so tempts, till we attain to read
The signs aright, and learn, by failure, truth is forced
To manifest itself through falsehood; whence divorced
By the excepted eye, at the rare season, for
The happy moment, truth instructs us to abhor
The false, and prize the true, obtainable thereby.
Then do we understand the value of a lie;
Its purpose served, its truth once safe deposited,
Each lie, superfluous now, leaves, in the singer's stead,
The indubitable song; the historic personage

Put by, leaves prominent the impulse of his age;
Truth sets aside speech, act, time, place, indeed, but brings
Nakedly forward now the principle of things
Highest and least."

CXXV

Wherewith change ends. What change to dread
When, disengaged at last from every veil, instead
Of type remains the truth? once—falsehood: but anon
Theosuton e broteion eper kekramenon,
Something as true as soul is true, though veils between
Prove false and fleet away. As I mean, did he mean,
The poet whose bird-phrase sits, singing in my ear
A mystery not unlike? What through the dark and drear
Brought comfort to the Titan? Emerging from the lymph,
"God, man, or mixture" proved only to be a nymph:
"From whom the clink on clink of metal" (money, judged
Abundant in my purse) "struck" (bumped at, till it budged)
"The modesty, her soul's habitual resident"
(Where late the sisterhood were lively in their tent)
"As out of wingèd car" (that caravan on wheels)
"Impulsively she rushed, no slippers to her heels,"
And "Fear not, friends we flock!" soft smiled the sea-Fifine—
Primitive of the veils (if he meant what I mean)
The poet's Titan learned to lift, ere "Three-formed Fate,
Moirai Trimorphoi" stood unmasked the Ultimate.

CXXVI

Enough o' the dream! You see how poetry turns prose.
Announcing wonder-work, I dwindle at the close
Down to mere commonplace old facts which everybody knows.
So dreaming disappoints! The fresh and strange at first,
Soon wears to trite and tame, nor warrants the outburst
Of heart with which we hail those heights, at very brink
Of heaven, whereto one least of lifts would lead, we think,
But wherefrom quick decline conducts our step, we find,
To homely earth, old facts familiar left behind.
Did not this monument, for instance, long ago
Say all it had to say, show all it had to show,
Nor promise to do duty more in dream?

CXXVII

Awaking so,
What if we, homeward-bound, all peace and some fatigue,
Trudge, soberly complete our tramp of near a league,
Last little mile which makes the circuit just, Elvire?
We end where we began: that consequence is clear.
All peace and some fatigue, wherever we were nursed
To life, we bosom us on death, find last is first
And thenceforth final too.

CXXVIII

"Why final? Why the more
Worth credence now than when such truth proved false before?"
Because a novel point impresses now: each lie
Redounded to the praise of man, was victory
Man's nature had both right to get, and might to gain,
And by no means implied submission to the reign
Of other quite as real a nature, that saw fit
To have its way with man, not man his way with it.
This time, acknowledgment and acquiescence quell
Their contrary in man; promotion proves as well
Defeat: and Truth, unlike the False with Truth's outside,
Neither plumes up his will nor puffs him out with pride.
I fancy, there must lurk some cogency i' the claim,
Man, such abatement made, submits to, all the same.
Soul finds no triumph, here, to register like Sense
With whom 't is ask and have,—the want, the evidence
That the thing wanted, soon or late, will be supplied.
This indeed plumes up will; this, sure, puffs out with pride,
When, reading records right, man's instincts still attest
Promotion comes to Sense because Sense likes it best;
For bodies sprouted legs, through a desire to run:
While hands, when fain to filch, got fingers one by one,
And nature, that 's ourself, accommodative brings
To bear that, tired of legs which walk, we now bud wings
Since of a mind to fly. Such savor in the nose
Of Sense would stimulate Soul sweetly, I suppose,
Soul with its proper itch of instinct, prompting clear
To recognize soul's self soul's only master here
Alike from first to last. But if time's pressure, light's
Or rather dark's approach, wrest thoroughly the rights
Of rule away, and bid the soul submissive bear
Another soul than it play master everywhere
In great and small,—this time, I fancy, none disputes
There 's something in the fact that such conclusion suits
Nowise the pride of man, nor yet chimes in with attributes
Conspicuous in the lord of nature. He receives

And not demands—not first likes faith and then believes.

CXXIX

And as with the last essence, so with its first faint type.
Inconstancy means raw, 't is faith alone means ripe
I' the soul which runs its round: no matter how it range
From Helen to Fifine, Elvire bids back the change
To permanence. Here, too, love ends where love began.
Such ending looks like law, because the natural man
Inclines the other way, feels lordlier free than bound.
Poor pabulum for pride when the first love is found
Last also! and, so far from realizing gain,
Each step aside just proves divergency in vain.
The wanderer brings home no profit from his quest
Beyond the sad surmise that keeping house were best
Could life begin anew. His problem posed aright
Was—"From the given point evolve the infinite!"
Not—"Spend thyself in space, endeavoring to joint
Together, and so make infinite, point and point:
Fix into one Elvire a Fair-ful of Fifines!"
Fifine, the foam-flake, she: Elvire, the sea's self, means
Capacity at need to shower how many such!
And yet we left her calm profundity, to clutch
Foam-flutter, bell on bell, that, bursting at a touch,
Blistered us for our pains. But wise, we want no more
O' the fickle element. Enough of foam and roar!
Land-locked, we live and die henceforth: for here 's the villa door.

CXXX

How pallidly you pause o' the threshold! Hardly night,
Which drapes you, ought to make real flesh and blood so white!
Touch me, and so appear alive to all intents!
Will the saint vanish from the sinner that repents?
Suppose you are a ghost! A memory, a hope,
A fear, a conscience! Quick! Give back the hand I grope
I' the dusk for!

CXXXI

That is well. Our double horoscope
I cast, while you concur. Discard that simile
O' the fickle element! Elvire is land not sea—
The solid land, the safe. All these word-bubbles came

O' the sea, and bite like salt. The unlucky bath's to blame.
This hand of yours on heart of mine, no more the bay
I beat, nor bask beneath the blue! In Pornic, say,
The Mayor shall catalogue me duly domiciled,
Contributable, good-companion of the guild
And mystery of marriage. I stickle for the town,
And not this tower apart; because, though, halfway down,
Its mullions wink o'erwebbed with bloomy greenness, yet
Who mounts to staircase top may tempt the parapet,
And sudden there 's the sea! No memories to arouse,
No fancies to delude! Our honest civic house
Of the earth be earthy too!—or graced perchance with shell
Made prize of long ago, picked haply where the swell
Menaced a little once—or seaweed-branch that yet
Dampens and softens, notes a freak of wind, a fret
Of wave: though, why on earth should sea-change mend or mar
The calm contemplative householders that we are?
So shall the seasons fleet, while our two selves abide:
E'en past astonishment how sunrise and springs tide
Could tempt one forth to swim; the more if time appoints
That swimming grow a task for one's rheumatic joints.
Such honest civic house, behold, I constitute
Our villa! Be but flesh and blood, and smile to boot!
Enter for good and all! then fate bolt fast the door,
Shut you and me inside, never to wander more!

CXXXII

Only,—you do not use to apprehend attack!
No doubt, the way I march, one idle arm, thrown slack
Behind me, leaves the open hand defenceless at the back,
Should an impertinent on tiptoe steal, and stuff
—Whatever can it be? A letter sure enough,
Pushed betwixt palm and glove! That largess of a franc?
Perhaps inconsciously,—to better help the blank
O' the nest, her tambourine, and, laying egg, persuade
A family to follow, the nest-egg that I laid
May have contained—but just to foil suspicious folk—
Between two silver whites a yellow double yolk!
Oh, threaten no farewell! five minutes shall suffice
To clear the matter up. I go, and in a trice
Return; five minutes past, expect me! If in vain—
Why, slip from flesh and blood, and play the ghost again!

EPILOGUE

THE HOUSEHOLDER

Savage I was sitting in my house, late, lone:
Dreary, weary with the long day's work:
Head of me, heart of me, stupid as a stone:
Tongue-tied now, now blaspheming like a Turk;
When, in a moment, just a knock, call, cry,
Half a pang and all a rapture, there again were we!—
"What, and is it really you again?" quoth I:
"I again, what else did you expect?" quoth She.

"Never mind, hie away from this old house—
Every crumbling brick embrowned with sin and shame!
Quick, in its corners ere certain shapes arouse!
Let them—every devil of the night—lay claim,
Make and mend, or rap and rend, for me! Good-by!
God be their guard from disturbance at their glee,
Till, crash, comes down the carcass in a heap!" quoth I:
"Nay, but there's a decency required!" quoth She.

"Ah, but if you knew how time has dragged, days, nights!
All the neighbor-talk with man and maid—such men!
All the fuss and trouble of street-sounds, window-sights:
All the worry of flapping door and echoing roof; and then,
All the fancies ... Who were they had leave, dared try
Darker arts that almost struck despair in me?
If you knew but how I dwelt down here!" quoth I:
"And was I so better off up there?" quoth She.

"Help and get it over! Reunited to his wife
(How draw up the paper lets the parish-people know?)
Lies M. or N., departed from this life,
Day the this or that, month and year the so and so.
What i' the way of final flourish? Prose, verse? Try!
Affliction sore long time he bore, or, what is it to be?
Till God did please to grant him ease. Do end!" quoth I:
"I end with—Love is all, and Death is naught!" quoth She.

Robert Browning – A Short Biography

He is the equal of any Victorian Poet that could be mentioned. However, Browning continues to be in the shadow of Tennyson, Arnold, Hopkins, Morris and many others.

Robert Browning was born on May 7th, 1812 in Walworth in the parish of Camberwell, London. He was baptized on June 14th, 1812, at Lock's Fields Independent Chapel, York Street, Walworth.

Browning's early years were certainly very interesting. His mother was an excellent pianist and a very devout evangelical Christian. His father, who worked as a clerk at the Bank of England, was also an artist, scholar, antiquarian, and collector of books and pictures. Indeed, he amassed more than 6,000 volumes of rare books including works in Greek, Hebrew, Latin, French, Italian, and Spanish. For the young and curious Browning, it was a wonderful resource, added to which his father was a guiding force in his education.

Many accounts attest that Browning was already proficient at reading and writing by the age of five. He is said to have been a bright but anxious student and to have studied and learnt Latin, Greek, and French by the time he was fourteen. From fourteen to sixteen he was educated at home, tutored in music, drawing, dancing, and horsemanship. Certainly, language and the arts were two areas the young Browning both absorbed and pushed himself towards.

At the age of twelve he wrote a volume of Byronic verse he called Incondita, which his parents attempted to have published. The attempts were unsuccessful and, disappointed, Browning destroyed the work.

In 1825, a cousin gave Browning a collection of Percy Bysshe Shelley's poetry; Browning was so enamored with the poems that he asked for the rest of Shelley's works for his thirteenth birthday. In fact, Browning then went the extra mile, declaring himself to be both a vegetarian and an atheist in honour of his hero.

Intriguingly it seems that the rejection of his first volume didn't dim his appreciation of other poets, but it appears to have stopped him writing any poems between the ages of thirteen and twenty.

In 1828, Browning enrolled at the newly-opened University of London. He was uncomfortable with the experience and he soon left, anxious to read and absorb at his own pace.

His education which, overall is notably rambling and lacks a structure that many of his artistic contemporaries enjoyed, i.e. excellent public schooling and then a degree at Oxford or Cambridge, may present many of his critics with ammunition to criticize, but alternatively his hap-hazard education certainly contributed to many of the references that baffled both critics and his audience, but they tellingly show the breath and scale of what he could turn words too. What others would call obscure references were, to Browning, remarkably obvious.

Browning's early career was very promising. His long poem Pauline (of which only a fragment was ever finished and published) brought him to the attention of the Pre-Raphaelite master Dante Gabriel Rossetti and his difficult Paracelsus (published in 1835) was warmly admired by both Dickens and Wordsworth.

In the 1830s he met the actor William Macready and was encouraged to develop and turn his talents to the stage by writing verse drama. But these plays, including Strafford, which ran for five nights in 1837, and those contained within the Bells and Pomegranates series, were, for the most part, unsuccessful.

During this period Browning began to discover that his real talents lay in taking a single character and allowing that character to discover more about himself by revealing further personal aspects of himself in his speeches; the dramatic monologue. The techniques he developed through this—especially the use of diction, rhythm, and symbol—are regarded as his most important contribution to poetry. They would later influence such major poets of the 20th Century as Ezra Pound, T. S. Eliot, and Robert Frost.

By 1840, with the publication of Sordello, the tide turned somewhat. Many thought he was being deliberately obscure, opaque beyond measure and his poetry for the next decade or so was not eagerly acquired or talked about.

As Browning attempted to rehabilitate his career he began a relationship with Elizabeth Barrett in 1845. He had read her poems and, being totally charmed by their quality, was determined to meet her. The poetess was better known than the younger Browning but suffered from a debilitating illness and was also subject to the harsh behaviour of her over-bearing father. Nevertheless, the new couple were soon inseparable.

Her father, as he did with any of his children that married, disinherited her. Despite this she had some money from her own resources and sensing that the best outcome for both the relationship and her own health was to move abroad the couple did just that. After a private marriage at St Marylebone Parish Church, in September 1846, they journeyed to Europe to honeymoon in Paris.

Their new life now took them to Italy, first to Pisa and a little later to Florence. There they absorbed life and one another.

But in the short term the literary assault on Browning's work did not let up. He was now criticized by such patrician writers as Charles Kingsley for his abandonment of England for foreign lands. Browning could do little to answer these attacks except to compose with his pen and continue with his poetical journey.

The Browning's were well respected, and even famous. Elizabeth health began to improve, she grew stronger and in 1849, at the age of 43, between four miscarriages, she gave birth to a son, Robert Wiedeman Barrett Browning, whom they nicknamed "Penini" or "Pen",

Intriguingly despite his growing reputation and return to form as a poet he was more often than not known as 'Elizabeth Barrett's husband'.

Work flowed from his pen that was to ensure his reputation as one of England's leading poets. When his collection Men and Women was published in 1855 it contained some of his finest lines. It was dedicated to Elizabeth. Life had begun to smile handsome rewards upon the Brownings.

Victorian society was very much taken with all things spiritualist. It was not enough to have command of much of the globe through Empire, they wished to know and explore wherever they could. The spirit world beckoned their interest. Browning dissented from this view believing it was all a hoax and a fraud. Elizabeth, however, was inclined to believe and this caused several disagreements between the couple.

They attended a séance by Daniel Dunglas Home, in July 1855. (Home was a famous and clamored after Scottish physical medium with the reported ability to levitate and speak with the dead). It is said that during this séance a spirit face materialised. Home then claimed it was the face of Browning's son who had died in infancy. Browning seized the 'materialisation' which turned out to be Home's bare foot. Browning had never lost a son in infancy.

After the séance, Browning wrote an angry letter to The Times, in which he said: "the whole display of hands, spirit utterances etc., was a cheat and imposture."

The Browning's time in Italy were immensely rewarding years for both their personal and professional lives. Browning encouraged her to include Sonnets from the Portuguese in her published works, these beautiful poems are undoubtedly one of the highlights of English love poetry.

Elizabeth had become quite politicised during these years. Engrossed in Italian politics (which was continuing to slowly re-unify the country), she issued a small volume of political poems entitled Poems before Congress (1860) most of which were written to express her sympathy with the Italian cause after the earlier outbreak of The Second Italian Independence War in 1859. In England they caused uproar. Conservative magazines such as Blackwood's and the Saturday Review labelled her a fanatic. She dedicated the book to her husband.

But in 1861 tragedy struck.

The couple had spent the winter of 1860–61 in Rome when Elizabeth's health deteriorated again and they returned to Florence in early June. However, these turned out to be her final weeks. Only morphine would now still the pain. She died in Browning's arms on June 29th, 1861. Browning said that she died "smilingly, happily, and with a face like a girl's .... Her last word was .... "Beautiful".

Her burial took place in the nearby Protestant English Cemetery of Florence. The local people were deeply saddened, and shops closed their doors in grief and respect.

Browning and their son were obviously devastated. Unable to bear being in Florence without Elizabeth they soon returned to London to live at 19 Warwick Crescent, Maida Vale.

As he re-integrated himself back into the London literary scene he began to finally receive the proper praise, respect and reputation that his works deserved.

Browning went on to publish Dramatis Personæ (1864), and The Ring and the Book (1868–1869). The latter, based on an "old yellow book" which told of a seventeenth-century Italian murder trial, received wide and generous critical acclaim. Although by now he was in the twilight of a long and prolific career, that had achieved some notable ups and downs, he was respected and indeed renowned for his talents and works.

In 1878, he revisited Italy for the first time since Elizabeth's death. He would return there on several further occasions but never to Florence.

Such was the esteem he was held in that The Browning Society was founded in 1881. Although he had never obtained a degree (something that set him apart from many other Victorian poets) he was now awarded honorary degrees from Oxford University in 1882 and then the University of Edinburgh in 1884.

In 1887, Browning produced the major work of his later years, Parleyings with Certain People of Importance in Their Day. Browning now spoke with his own voice as he engaged in a series of dialogues with long-forgotten figures of literary, artistic, and philosophic history. Unfortunately, both the critics and public were completely baffled by this.

On April 7th, 1889 Browning attended a dinner party at the home of his friend, the artist Rudolf Lehmann. The highlight of which was a recording made on a wax cylinder on an Edison cylinder phonograph. On the recording, which still exists, Browning recites part of How They Brought the Good News from Ghent to Aix, and can even be heard apologising when he forgets the words.

The recording was first played in 1890 on the anniversary of his death, at a gathering of his admirers, it was said to be the first time anyone's voice 'had been heard from beyond the grave'.

His last work Asolando: Fancies and Facts (1889), returned to his brief and concise lyric verse that was so popular. It was published on the day of his death on December 12th, 1889, Robert Browning was at his son's home Ca' Rezzonico in Venice.

He was buried in Poets' Corner in Westminster Abbey; his grave lies immediately adjacent to that of Alfred Tennyson.

Among the many who have publicly acknowledged their literary debt to him are Henry James, Oscar Wilde, George Bernard Shaw, G. K. Chesterton, Ezra Pound, Jorge Luis Borges, and Vladimir Nabokov.

Robert Browning - A Concise Bibliography

Here follows a list of the plays and poetry volumes published during his lifetime. Poems of particular worth are noted from within those volumes.

Pauline: A Fragment of a Confession (1833)
Paracelsus (1835)
Strafford (play) (1837)
Sordello (1840)
Bells and Pomegranates No. I: Pippa Passes (play) (1841)
 The Year's at the Spring
Bells and Pomegranates No. II: King Victor and King Charles (play) (1842)
Bells and Pomegranates No. III: Dramatic Lyrics (1842)
 Porphyria's Lover
 Soliloquy of the Spanish Cloister
 My Last Duchess
 The Pied Piper of Hamelin
 Count Gismond
 Johannes Agricola in Meditation
Bells and Pomegranates No. IV: The Return of the Druses (play) (1843)
Bells and Pomegranates No. V: A Blot in the 'Scutcheon (play) (1843)
Bells and Pomegranates No. VI: Colombe's Birthday (play) (1844)
Bells and Pomegranates No. VII: Dramatic Romances and Lyrics (1845)
 The Laboratory
 How They Brought the Good News from Ghent to Aix
 The Bishop Orders His Tomb at Saint Praxed's Church
 The Lost Leader
 Home Thoughts from Abroad

www.ingramcontent.com/pod-product-compliance
Lightning Source LLC
Chambersburg PA
CBHW060146050426
42448CB00010B/2326